A Journey with John

The 50 Day Bible Challenge

ISBN: 978-0-88028-436-3

Printed in USA

A Journey with John

The 50 Day Bible Challenge

Edited by Marek P. Zabriskie

FORWARD MOVEMENT
Cincinnati, Ohio

To Mims, for all your patience and support—
a faithful Bible reader, wife, and fantastic mother

Preface

The Bible Challenge began as a simple idea: to encourage daily reading of scripture. Simple ideas can bring forth great change.

Developing a daily spiritual discipline or practice is crucial for all Christians who wish to be faithful followers of Jesus. Saint Augustine and many other great Christians have written about the power of reading the Bible quietly on our own. There is no other book in the world that can so transform the human heart, motivate the human spirit, and give us the mind that was in Christ Jesus himself.

The Bible remains the world's best-selling book year after year. However, Episcopalians, Roman Catholics, and other mainline Christians often do not read it. Church historian and author Diana Butler Bass reports that among the 22,000 Christian groups and denominations in the United States, Episcopalians are the best-educated group but drop to nearly last when it comes to biblical literacy.

The goal of The Bible Challenge is to help individuals develop a lifelong, daily spiritual discipline of reading the Bible so that their lives may be constantly transformed and renewed. Studies reveal that prayerfully engaging scripture is the best way for Christians to grow in their faith and love of Jesus.

More than 500,000 persons in 2,500 churches in over fifty countries are now participating in The Bible Challenge. We continue our partnership with Forward Movement with this new series—a focus on reading one book of the Bible over a fifty-day period. This book joins *A Journey with Matthew, A Journey with Mark,* and *A Journey with Luke* to complete the gospel series. This Bible Challenge series is an ideal resource for individuals, churches, and dioceses during the Easter season or any time of the year.

Regular engagement with the Bible develops a strong Christian faith, enhances our experience of worship, and helps to create a more committed, articulate, and contagious Christian. This is exactly what the world needs today.

With prayers and blessings for your faithful Bible reading,

The Rev. Marek P. Zabriskie
Founder of The Bible Challenge
Director of the Center for Biblical Studies
www.thecenterforbiblicalstudies.org
Rector of St. Thomas' Episcopal Church
Fort Washington, Pennsylvania

How to Read the Bible Prayerfully

Welcome to The 50 Day Bible Challenge. We are delighted that you are interested in reading God's life-transforming Word from the Gospel of John. It will change and enrich your life. Here are some suggestions to consider as you get started:

- You can begin The 50 Day Bible Challenge at any time of year. It works especially well for the fifty days of Eastertide, beginning on Easter Day. It also could be read during Lent, beginning on the Sunday before Ash Wednesday.
- Each day has a manageable amount of reading, a meditation, a question or two, and a prayer, written by a host of wonderful authors.
- We suggest that you try to read the Bible each day. This is a great spiritual discipline to establish.
- If you need more than fifty days to read through the Gospel of John, we support you in moving at the pace that works best for you.
- Many Bible Challenge participants read the Bible using their iPad, iPhone, Kindle, or Nook, or listen to the Bible on CDs or on a mobile device using Audio.com, faithcomesthroughhearing.org, or Pandora radio. Find what works for you.
- Other resources for learning more about the Bible and engaging scripture can be found on our website, ForwardMovement.org. In addition, you can find a list of resources at thecenterforbiblicalresources.org. The center also offers a Read the Bible in a Year program and reading plans for the New Testament, Psalms, and Proverbs.

- Because the Bible is not a newspaper, it is best to read it with a reverent spirit. We advocate a devotional approach to reading the Bible, rather than reading it as a purely intellectual or academic exercise.
- Before reading the Bible, take a moment of silence to put yourself in the presence of God. We then invite you to read this prayer written by Archbishop Thomas Cranmer.

  Blessed Lord, who has caused all holy scriptures to be written for our learning: Grant us to hear them, read, mark, learn, and inwardly digest them, that we may embrace and ever hold fast the blessed hope of everlasting life, which you have given us in our Savior Jesus Christ; who lives and reigns with you and the Holy Spirit, one God, for ever and ever. Amen.
- Consider using the ancient monastic practice of *lectio divina*. In this form of Bible reading, you read the text and then meditate on a portion of it—be it a verse or two or even a single word. Mull over the words and their meaning. Then offer a prayer to God based on what you have read, how it has made you feel, or what it has caused you to ponder. Listen in silence for God to respond to your prayer.
- We encourage you to read in the morning, if possible, so that your prayerful reading may spiritually enliven the rest of your day. If you cannot read in the morning, read when you can later in the day. Try to carve out a regular time for your daily reading.
- One way to hold yourself accountable to reading God's Word is to form a group within your church or community. By participating in The 50 Day Bible Challenge together,

you can support one another in your reading, discuss the Bible passages, ask questions, and share how God's Word is transforming your life.

- If you do not want to join a group, you may wish to invite a friend or family member (or two) to share The 50 Day Bible Challenge with you.
- Ask to have a notice printed in your church newsletter that you are starting a group to participate in *The 50 Day Bible Challenge*. Invite others to join you and to gather regularly to discuss the readings, ask questions, and share how they are transforming your life. Visit the Center for Biblical Resources website to see more suggestions about how churches can participate in The Bible Challenge.
- If you form a Bible Challenge group, you might consider holding a gathering or meal to celebrate your spiritual accomplishment.
- Have fun and find spiritual peace and the joy that God desires for you in your daily reading. The goal of the Center for Biblical Studies is to help you discover God's wisdom and to create a lifelong spiritual practice of daily Bible reading so that God may guide you through each day of your life.
- If you find reading the entire Bible and being part of The Bible Challenge to be a blessing in your life, then we strongly encourage you to share the blessing. Invite several friends or family members to participate in The Bible Challenge.
- Once you've finished one complete reading of the Bible, start over and do it again. God may speak differently to

you in each reading. Follow the example of U.S. President John Adams, who read through the Bible each year during his adult life. We highly advocate this practice.

- After participating in The 50 Day Bible Challenge, you will be more equipped to support and mentor others in reading the Bible.

We are thrilled that you are participating in The Bible Challenge. May God richly bless you as you prayerfully engage the scriptures each day.

An Introduction to the Gospel of John

My introduction to the Gospel of John came in a most unexpected way: watching an Atlanta Braves baseball game. Someone in the outfield bleachers held a large sign that read "John 3:16." Even as a baptized and confirmed Episcopalian, I had never read the Bible. I had not actively attended church since I was confirmed as a teenager.

At first, I thought that John 3:16 might be a lopsided baseball score, but that seemed odd. I turned and asked a friend about it. He explained that John 3:16 was one of the most famous verses in the entire Bible, and then he quoted it to me: "For God so loved the world that he gave his only Son, so that everyone who believes in him may not perish but may have eternal life." I was impressed that he could recite the passage by heart and figured that it must be important. Still, its significance fell on deaf ears.

Later, this same friend invited me to join a Bible study that met at the fraternity house. Although it seemed like an odd place to explore Christianity, we sat in his room and talked about John's Gospel. Then he asked me to read a portion of the first chapter aloud. I had never actually opened a Bible, let alone read it. That was a moment I will never forget.

I had hardly lived an angelic life up to that point, and as I read aloud from the Bible, I felt as if I was standing before God. At times my mind drifted to my fraternity brothers nearby. I tried to suppress my laughter, knowing that if they could see me reading the Bible in the fraternity house that had the most notorious reputation on campus, they would split their sides laughing. But God got my attention—and would not let go—and I read the entire gospel. I fell in love with it.

Many years later, the Gospel of Luke is my favorite. Yet I find John's Gospel extremely refreshing, enjoyable, and enlightening to read. My practice is to read through the Bible every year, which leads me to read the four gospels in this traditional order: Matthew, Mark, Luke, and John. There are such great similarities between the first three that I always eagerly look forward to reading John, because the Fourth Gospel is distinctively different from the others.

During my first years as a priest, the Rev. Julian Gunn was kind enough to teach me how to read the Bible in Greek. We began with John, which is probably the easiest book in the New Testament to read in ancient Greek. As we read together, my love of John deepened. And thankfully, so did my knowledge of Greek, although I'm grateful for the gospel's repeated use of certain words like look, see, witness, believe, glory, and abide.

John's Gospel is fairly short, composed of around 15,000 words. (In comparison, Luke is the longest gospel, with about 19,500 words). Like most ancient biographies, John is not a full chronicling of a person's life but rather offers significant stories about its subject, that is, Jesus. The Fourth Gospel also belongs to the "Johannine works," which include the epistles of John and Revelation.

The Gospel of John is broken into four major pieces. The first part (1:1-18) is the Prologue and serves to set forth themes that will be explored in the gospel. The section from 1:19—12:50 is called the Book of Signs, featuring Jesus' public miracles that point like signs to his divine nature. The third section, the Book of Glory (13:1—20:31), covers the last few days before the crucifixion, as Jesus teaches his disciples and bids them farewell. John's Gospel culminates with Jesus' death and resurrection, revealing the glory of God. The final verses (21:1-25) show how Peter is restored to leadership after having denied Jesus.

At first glance, John's Gospel may seem the most straightforward of the gospels, but John also reveals a host of deeper messages. It is the most poetic and mystical of all the gospels, steeped in Hebrew scriptures and Jewish beliefs and worship. Many of the important stories are told against the background of the Jewish Passover, the feasts of Tabernacles, Hanukkah, and the Sabbath.

Within John's Gospel, we find the highest Christology of Jesus found in the New Testament: Jesus is clearly the Son of God. He is fully divine, speaking as no human has ever spoken (7:46). John's Christology is clear. He wants us to know that "Jesus is the Christ, the Son of God" (20:31). God is called Father more than a hundred times in the Fourth Gospel, and Jesus is referred to as "Son" about fifty times. This high Christology of Jesus is reflected in the great "I am" statements. The highest salutation to God in the Old Testament is found in Exodus 3:14 when God says, "I AM WHO I AM." John's Gospel works off this salutation from Exodus as Jesus makes his seven "I am" statements, found between chapters 6 and 15, claiming to be the bread of life, the light of the world, the door of the sheepfold, the good shepherd, the resurrection and the life, the way, the truth and the life, and the true vine.

While John underplays Jesus' suffering on the cross, he also offers a very human portrayal of Christ, making it clear that in Jesus, God was "made flesh" (1:14). In John's Gospel, Jesus becomes exhausted (4:6), he suffers anguish (12:27; 13:21), and he weeps profoundly over Lazarus' death (11:33-35). Jesus changes his mind (7:1-10) and displays irritation (2:4; 6:26; 7:6-8; 8:25). Jesus has certain disciples that he prefers over others, and he bonds with those who follow him, calling his followers "friends."

The symbol of John's Gospel is the eagle. The ancients believed that the eagle was the only bird that could soar directly into the sun and not be blinded by the light, enabling it to soar higher than any other bird. Twentieth-century theologian William Barclay proclaims that John takes us higher and closer to God than the other three gospels, Matthew, Mark, and Luke. They are known as the Synoptic Gospels; *syn-optic* comes from the Greek word meaning capable of being "seen together." John's Gospel is different, portraying Jesus speaking in monologues, exuding brilliant flashes of light, truth, and inspiration. Jesus does not speak in aphorisms or tell parables nor does he burst into attacks on the Pharisees and Sadducees. Instead, John recounts Jesus giving long, meditative discourses. His wondrous actions are not called "miracles" but rather "signs" (*semeia*) that reveal God's glory.

John's Gospel portrays Jesus' ministry extending over a three-year period, whereas the Synoptic Gospels depict his ministry taking place in one year. Another key difference is that the Last Supper is not a Passover, and instead, in John, Jesus' death takes place on the day of preparation for Passover.

In addition, locations of events in John's account are different from those in the Synoptic Gospels. In John, Jesus spends most of his time in Jerusalem and Judea, with only occasional withdrawals to Galilee. In *Readings in St. John's Gospel*, Archbishop of Canterbury William Temple explains that John's chronology of Jesus' ministry is more detailed and makes more sense than those of the Synoptic Gospels. How could Jesus have made preparations for the Triumphal Entry and the Last Supper if he hadn't been to Jerusalem since boyhood? What did it mean for Jesus to cry bitterly over the city saying, "How often I would have gathered your children," unless he had made several missionary visits there? Perhaps because of John's focus on chronology and location, the common lectionary shared by Episcopalians, Lutherans, Roman Catholics, Methodists, and Presbyterians does not set aside a year to read the Gospel of John. Whereas each of the Synoptic Gospels have set years for reading, parts of John's Gospel are read aloud over three years and help fill in parts of the story.

John alone tells of the marriage feast in Cana in chapter two (mentioned in many Episcopal wedding services); of the coming of Nicodemus (3:1-15); of the Samaritan woman (4); of the raising of Lazarus (11); and of Jesus' washing the disciples' feet (13:1-17). Only in John does Jesus offer his wonderful teaching about the Holy Spirit and discuss sending an Advocate to his disciples (chapters 14-17). Even more significantly, the cleansing of the temple occurs early in John's Gospel—a key act leading authorities to view Jesus as a threat and take decisive action to kill him. He also notes that Jesus' sole Galilean appearance after his crucifixion took place at a seaside location, as opposed to a mountaintop. And only John has Mary Magdalene coming to the tomb alone, discovering that Jesus' body is missing. While John is home to some of these sacred, oft-explored stories, there is no account in the Fourth Gospel of Jesus' temptation or of the Last Supper, nothing about Gethsemane or Jesus' Ascension.

Another major difference that can appear quite disturbing in John's Gospel is that John refers to "the Jews" seventy-five times. This has led some to suggest that John's Gospel is anti-Semitic. I believe that for John though, "the Jews" represent all humans who choose to reject God's truth. In this sense, any of us who choose not to believe

Jesus' message, who have decided not to follow his light and truth, are turning from God. At the same time, John also explicitly calls Jesus "a Jew," noting that salvation is "from the Jews" (4:9, 22).

Given these differences, many scholars believe John was written independently of the Synoptics. So who was the author of John's Gospel? Like each of the other canonical gospels, there is much speculation as to who wrote the Fourth Gospel. Irenaeus, an early Church Father, tells us that John was a disciple of Jesus Christ who wrote from Ephesus, an important city in biblical times. Some speculate the author was the anonymous disciple identified in the text as the one "whom Jesus loved" (13:23; 19:26, 20:2-9). While no one named John is mentioned in the gospel, some believe that the author John was one of the sons of Zebedee. (And the Synoptic Gospels tell us that Zebedee indeed had a son named John).

If John, son of Zebedee, or the Beloved Disciple wrote the Fourth Gospel, then the author was clearly an eyewitness to Jesus' ministry. Regardless of the author, the Fourth Gospel was the last to be written down—sometime near the end of the first century, and the audience had changed. Within thirty years after Jesus died, Christianity had spread rapidly to Greece and Asia Minor and began to flourish in Rome. Greeks and Greek-speaking converts to the faith greatly outnumbered Jewish converts, which raised a major question about how to present a Jewish religious experience to Gentile Christians. The Christian church was overwhelmingly Gentile by the time John's Gospel was written, and so it restates Christianity for a Hellenistic audience. For instance, Greeks were not familiar with genealogies, and John was writing for a primarily Greek audience. So, while Matthew and Luke provide an infancy narrative and genealogies for Jesus, John introduces us to Jesus as a fully grown adult.

There are signs that John's Gospel was altered over time. Some scholars claim that as many as five revisions took place before the gospel appeared in the form that we have now. So why was John's Gospel written? Some say that it was to prove the superiority of Jesus over John the Baptist, to demonstrate the exceptional credentials of Jesus to those who were following John the Baptist. Whenever John the Baptist appears in the Fourth Gospel, he points people toward Jesus, making it clear that Jesus "is the light of the world." The Fourth Gospel may have been written for members of the Jewish Diaspora or those who had shown an openness to Jesus' message and had not been expelled from synagogues. Clement of Alexandria said that John was a "spiritual gospel," written to supplement the historical and physical facts of the three other gospels. Indeed, throughout the gospel, John focuses on very simple things such as birth, water, sight, and bread and imbues them with deep themes and motifs. John calls us to move beyond the superficial nature of things into their deeper spiritual reality, such as when Jesus speaks of the "true bread" or the "true vine."

There is probably no single reason why this gospel was written, and it was clearly not written for one single audience. The author may give us the best indication of the intention:

> Now Jesus did many other signs in the presence of the disciples, which are not written in this book. But these are written so that you may come to believe that Jesus is the Messiah, the Son of God, and that through believing you may have life in his name (20:30-31).

This statement makes clear that the purpose of the gospel is conversion. Throughout the gospel, John forces the reader to make choices between light and darkness, truth and falsehood, good and evil, heaven and hell. The reader must choose one or the other—there are no sidelines to sit on, safely divorced from the action. Each reader is pushed to make choices along the way—to a side with or against Jesus and his message.

In this sense, John's Gospel displays what scholars call a "realized eschatology"—the kingdom of God can be found here and now as opposed to only being apprehended and experienced in the life to come. For John, the end of time is a present reality: Jesus says, "the time is coming and now is" (4:23, 5:25). Even Lazarus is raised from the dead now, rather than waiting for the end time. Still, John recalls Jesus talking about "the last day" as a time when God's final judgment will take place—and a reminder that Christians then—and now—are only experiencing glimpses of heaven on earth.

One final note about the Gospel of John: It elucidates the idea of "the Word," as it is known by the Jews, or the divine *logos*, in Greek. The Word of God is living and has the power to make things happen, to bring about change. John's first verse proclaims, "In the beginning was the Word, and the Word was with God, and the Word was God." This echoes the prophet Isaiah, who writes, "so shall my word be that goes out from my mouth; it shall not return to me empty, but it shall accomplish that which I purpose, and succeed in the thing for which I sent it" (55:11). Jeremiah adds, "Is not my word like fire, says the Lord, and like a hammer that breaks a rock in pieces?" (23:29).

And of course, the opening verse of John's Gospel hearkens back to the first passage in the Bible, where we read, "In the beginning..." John's opening suggests that Christ preexists creation and is with God the Father and the Holy Spirit at the creation of all things. Like a composer who begins a musical score by echoing the great themes to follow, John highlights light and life—two of the great themes of his gospel.

The essays that follow by bishops, biblical scholars, theologians, writers, chaplains, professors, cathedral deans, and parish priests offer a rich array of insights into the light and life of Christ, as seen through the lens of the Gospel of John. Forward Movement and I are extremely grateful for their words, and we hope that you find their offerings inspiring and engaging.

I began reading John's Gospel in a most unlikely place and discovered a compelling, convicting spiritual narrative that helped me grow in faith. May you enjoy doing the same with the guidance of this book.

With peace and joy,

Marek

A Journey with John

The 50 Day Bible Challenge

Day 1

John 1:1-18

1 In the beginning was the
Word, and the Word was
with God, and the Word was
God. 2He was in the beginning
with God. 3All things came into
being through him, and without
him not one thing came into
being. What has come into being
4in him was life, and the life was
the light of all people. 5The light
shines in the darkness, and the
darkness did not overcome it.

6There was a man sent from God,
whose name was John. 7He came
as a witness to testify to the light,
so that all might believe through
him. 8He himself was not the
light, but he came to testify to
the light. 9The true light, which
enlightens everyone, was coming
into the world.

10He was in the world, and the
world came into being through
him; yet the world did not know
him. 11He came to what was his
own, and his own people did
not accept him. 12But to all who
received him, who believed in his
name, he gave power to become
children of God, 13who were
born, not of blood or of the will
of the flesh or of the will of man,
but of God.

14And the Word became flesh
and lived among us, and we have
seen his glory, the glory as of a
father's only son, full of grace
and truth. 15(John testified to
him and cried out, "This was
he of whom I said, 'He who
comes after me ranks ahead of
me because he was before me.'")
16From his fullness we have all
received, grace upon grace. 17The
law indeed was given through
Moses; grace and truth came
through Jesus Christ. 18No one
has ever seen God. It is God the
only Son, who is close to the
Father's heart, who has made
him known.

Reflection

Where does the story of Jesus start? Mark begins with Jesus' baptism in the Jordan, Matthew with his birth, and Luke with John the Baptist's prophesy, but the Gospel of John takes us right back to "in the beginning," with God himself before all time and space. John's Prologue is more like an overture, introducing all the great themes that will follow in this gospel.

John does not name Jesus, preferring to call him "the Word" (*logos*). This draws on Greek ideas of the logical rationality behind the cosmos as well as Jewish beliefs about God's Wisdom at creation bringing everything into existence through spoken word. Jesus is the source of all life and the true light that enlightens everyone.

And yet Jesus humbles himself to become human and to pitch his tent among us, sharing our existence, revealing the God whom no human being has ever seen. In this extraordinary life of the carpenter from Nazareth, God manifests his glory, full of grace and truth—and makes us his children.

Despite this, there are those who prefer not to know or accept him, so God sends people to witness for him. Thus there is an inevitable choice: Do we see Christ's glory, receive his life, and share it with others, or do we prefer to remain in the darkness? Here, with the Word made flesh, we can know truth and receive grace, light, and life—all else is death.

The Rev. Canon Professor Richard A. Burridge
Dean of King's College London and
Professor of Biblical Interpretation
London, England

Questions

How can we enable people to find God manifested in Jesus Christ dwelling among us today? Do we reflect his glory, light, and truth in our lives? Will we dare to follow his example of entering so fully into humanity that others will see the revelation of God's divine life shining through?

Prayer

God our Father, inspire with your Holy Spirit our study of these written words that we may know and love your living Word, Jesus Christ. *Amen.*

DAY 2

John 1:19-34

[19]This is the testimony given by John when the Jews sent priests and Levites from Jerusalem to ask him, “Who are you?” [20]He confessed and did not deny it, but confessed, “I am not the Messiah.” [21]And they asked him, “What then? Are you Elijah?” He said, “I am not.” “Are you the prophet?” He answered, “No.” [22]Then they said to him, “Who are you? Let us have an answer for those who sent us. What do you say about yourself?” [23]He said, “I am the voice of one crying out in the wilderness, ‘Make straight the way of the Lord,’” as the prophet Isaiah said.

[24]Now they had been sent from the Pharisees. [25]They asked him, “Why then are you baptizing if you are neither the Messiah, nor Elijah, nor the prophet?” [26]John answered them, “I baptize with water. Among you stands one whom you do not know, [27]the one who is coming after me; I am not worthy to untie the thong of his sandal.” [28]This took place in Bethany across the Jordan where John was baptizing.

[29]The next day he saw Jesus coming toward him and declared, “Here is the Lamb of God who takes away the sin of the world! [30]This is he of whom I said, ‘After me comes a man who ranks ahead of me because he was before me.’ [31]I myself did not know him; but I came baptizing with water for this reason, that he might be revealed to Israel.” [32]And John testified, “I saw the Spirit descending from heaven like a dove, and it remained on him. [33]I myself did not know him, but the one who sent me to baptize with water said to me, ‘He on whom you see the Spirit descend and remain is the one who baptizes with the Holy Spirit.’ [34]And I myself have seen and have testified that this is the Son of God.”

Reflection

As the strains of John's overture fade, the curtain rises, and the story begins. But the main character is curiously off-stage. Instead, the "witness" mentioned in the Prologue continues to introduce the main themes about who Jesus is.

John's baptisms in the Jordan bring him to the attention of the religious authorities in Jerusalem, who then send people to question him. This is the first appearance of the phrase "the Jews," which occurs frequently in this gospel. We must remember that John the Baptist was Jewish, as were Jesus, the disciples, the crowds, and the author himself. Since John uses "the Jews" as shorthand for Jesus' questioners and opponents, we must understand this to refer to the religious authorities rather than the entire Jewish community.

In response to the religious authorities, John insists three times that he is not the Christ nor a prophet like Elijah—merely the "voice of one crying in the wilderness," baptizing people and preparing the way of a greater One yet to come. When Jesus briefly appears, there is no account of him being baptized. Instead, John again bears witness, directing attention away from himself to Jesus, the Lamb of God who takes away the sin of the world, who "baptizes with the Holy Spirit." In fact, Jesus is nothing less than the Son of God.

Following John's lead, our job is to direct people to the extraordinary person who has come among us, to take away our sin, to reveal God, and to bring us back to right relationship with our Creator and Redeemer.

The Rev. Canon Professor Richard A. Burridge
Dean of King's College London and
Professor of Biblical Interpretation
London, England

Questions

Do we like to be the center of attention, attracting notice and being questioned by others? How can we deflect attention from ourselves and witness to what Jesus means to us? How might we translate biblical phrases like "Lamb of God" or "baptism in the Spirit" for others today?

Prayer

Lord, make us a voice crying aloud and direct others away from ourselves that they may see you and find in you forgiveness, life, and truth. *Amen.*

DAY 3

John 1:35-51

35The next day John again was
standing with two of his disciples,
36and as he watched Jesus walk
by, he exclaimed, "Look, here is
the Lamb of God!" 37The two
disciples heard him say this, and
they followed Jesus. 38When Jesus
turned and saw them following,
he said to them, "What are
you looking for?" They said to
him, "Rabbi" (which translated
means Teacher), "where are you
staying?" 39He said to them,
"Come and see." They came and
saw where he was staying, and
they remained with him that day.
It was about four o'clock in the
afternoon. 40One of the two who
heard John speak and followed
him was Andrew, Simon Peter's
brother. 41He first found his
brother Simon and said to him,
"We have found the Messiah"
(which is translated Anointed).
42He brought Simon to Jesus,
who looked at him and said,
"You are Simon son of John. You
are to be called Cephas" (which
is translated Peter).

43The next day Jesus decided to go
to Galilee. He found Philip and
said to him, "Follow me." 44Now
Philip was from Bethsaida,
the city of Andrew and Peter.
45Philip found Nathanael and
said to him, "We have found
him about whom Moses in
the law and also the prophets
wrote, Jesus son of Joseph from
Nazareth." 46Nathanael said
to him, "Can anything good
come out of Nazareth?" Philip
said to him, "Come and see."
47When Jesus saw Nathanael
coming toward him, he said of
him, "Here is truly an Israelite
in whom there is no deceit!"
48Nathanael asked him, "Where
did you get to know me?" Jesus
answered, "I saw you under the
fig tree before Philip called you."

[49]Nathanael replied, "Rabbi, you
are the Son of God! You are the
King of Israel!" [50]Jesus answered,
"Do you believe because I told
you that I saw you under the fig
tree? You will see greater things
than these." [51]And he said to
him, "Very truly, I tell you, you
will see heaven opened and the
angels of God ascending and
descending upon the Son of
Man."

Reflection

All four gospels emphasize Jesus' call to his first disciples to follow him. But only in John are we invited into the dynamic of the disciples' response. Some, like Nathanael, are suspicious and hesitant. Some respond with alacrity and immediately recruit their brothers and friends. Even the first ones to follow Jesus do not do so at his invitation but because of the witness of John the Baptist: "Look, here is the Lamb of God!"

The disorderliness and variability in these reactions to Jesus strikes me as very true to life. Most of us come to Jesus through the witness of others. Some of us are ready to follow him without hesitation. Others of us may believe that who he is and what he offers is too good to be true. It is unlikely that we would dismiss Jesus, as Nathanael did at first, because he came from a marginal and despised place. We have the opposite problem: Jesus' credentials are so impeccable that we don't feel we have the right to question his authority in our lives.

If we have a problem with Jesus, it is probably because we associate him with religious institutions that have abused power or substituted social status for radical witness. Can we admit and acknowledge that Jesus sees our bitterness and suspicion—and loves us for it? He sees and knows each of us, just as he saw and knew Nathanael under the fig tree.

The Rt. Rev. Thomas E. Breidenthal
Bishop of the Episcopal Diocese of Southern Ohio
Cincinnati, Ohio

Questions

In John, the call to follow Jesus does not come from him initially but through the agency of others. What does this say about our need to talk about Jesus with one another? Jesus literally renames Simon as Cephas (Peter) or "the Rock" and names Nathanael as an Israelite without guile. What is the centrally true and good thing about you that you think or hope Jesus would identify or name?

Prayer

Dear Jesus, you call us each by name and know us better than we know ourselves: Help us to trust you and to follow where you lead, who with the Father and the Holy Spirit live and reign, this day and always. *Amen.*

DAY 4

John 2:1-12

2 On the third day there was a
wedding in Cana of Galilee,
and the mother of Jesus was
there. 2Jesus and his disciples
had also been invited to the
wedding. 3When the wine gave
out, the mother of Jesus said to
him, "They have no wine." 4And
Jesus said to her, "Woman, what
concern is that to you and to me?
My hour has not yet come." 5His
mother said to the servants, "Do
whatever he tells you." 6Now
standing there were six stone
water jars for the Jewish rites
of purification, each holding
twenty or thirty gallons. 7Jesus
said to them, "Fill the jars with
water." And they filled them up
to the brim. 8He said to them,
"Now draw some out, and take
it to the chief steward." So they
took it. 9When the steward tasted
the water that had become wine,
and did not know where it came
from (though the servants who
had drawn the water knew), the
steward called the bridegroom
10and said to him, "Everyone
serves the good wine first, and
then the inferior wine after the
guests have become drunk. But
you have kept the good wine
until now." 11Jesus did this, the
first of his signs, in Cana of
Galilee, and revealed his glory;
and his disciples believed in him.

12After this he went down to
Capernaum with his mother, his
brothers, and his disciples; and
they remained there a few days.

Reflection

Throughout the gospels, Jesus is portrayed as a man who rejoices in celebrations and is quick to share occasions of joy with all sorts of people. John wastes no time in driving this point home. Jesus is at a wedding, and by his very presence teaches that the bonds of affection and mutual covenant that bind us together at so many levels—marriage, friendship, neighborhood, citizenship, treaty, and general good will—are blessed by God and invoke God's presence and nurture.

We are made for community, and Jesus constantly calls us into deeper community. But very often conviviality runs dry, and friendship sours. That is exactly why, when we are planning an important social event, we dread nothing more than running out of food or wine: They are the very symbols of continuing relationship with one another.

When Jesus turns water at this wedding into wine, he is demonstrating that he wants the celebration to continue and will sustain us in our life together. As with the parable of the loaves and fish, the resource for this sustenance does not come out of nowhere. Jesus uses the water that is at hand in the jars for purification. So it is in our marriages, friendships, parishes, neighborhoods: The raw materials for renewed connection and celebration are already in our midst. Rather than panicking about our capacity to carry on as communities of faith and practice, we should reflect on what it means that Jesus is already a guest at the party and has scoped out where the resources for renewal are to be found.

The Rt. Rev. Thomas E. Breidenthal
Bishop of the Episcopal Diocese of Southern Ohio
Cincinnati, Ohio

Questions

Where are you afraid the wine has run out in your communities or in your relationships? What is the water that is ready to be turned into wine? What assets stand ready to be not only tapped but also reimagined?

Prayer

Lord Jesus, your blessed mother urged you at Cana to turn water into wine: Inspire in us a spirit of urgency to invoke your action in our midst, that you, who know our needs before we ask, may help us see what is ripe for transformation. In your name we ask it. *Amen.*

DAY 5

John 2:13-25

[13]The Passover of the Jews
was near, and Jesus went up
to Jerusalem. [14]In the temple
he found people selling cattle,
sheep, and doves, and the money
changers seated at their tables.
[15]Making a whip of cords, he
drove all of them out of the
temple, both the sheep and the
cattle. He also poured out the
coins of the money changers and
overturned their tables. [16]He told
those who were selling the doves,
"Take these things out of here!
Stop making my Father's house
a marketplace!" [17]His disciples
remembered that it was written,
"Zeal for your house will
consume me." [18]The Jews then
said to him, "What sign can you
show us for doing this?" [19]Jesus
answered them, "Destroy this
temple, and in three days I will
raise it up." [20]The Jews then said,
"This temple has been under
construction for forty-six years,
and will you raise it up in three
days?" [21]But he was speaking of
the temple of his body. [22]After
he was raised from the dead, his
disciples remembered that he
had said this; and they believed
the scripture and the word that
Jesus had spoken.

[23]When he was in Jerusalem
during the Passover festival,
many believed in his name
because they saw the signs that
he was doing. [24]But Jesus on his
part would not entrust himself to
them, because he knew all people
[25]and needed no one to testify
about anyone; for he himself
knew what was in everyone.

Reflection

Jesus' cleansing of the temple is an episode recorded in all four gospels, but John treats it quite differently. First, he places it at the beginning of Jesus' ministry, not near the end as the other three do. Matthew, Mark, and Luke make this episode the deciding factor that leads the religious authorities to seek his death; John makes the cleansing of the temple an opening sign of what Jesus' ministry is all about.

The details in John's version are key. The listing of cattle, sheep, and doves shows what big business animal sacrifice had become, despite the strictures against this in the Hebrew scriptures. The reference to money changers alerts us to the way in which cash from Gentiles was laundered to make it suitably pure for use as an offering. Jesus' actions are clearly not intended to change all of this but to send an intentional message—to give a sign.

Jesus' answer to questioning by the religious authorities points them in a deeply theological direction. The temple where God ought to be encountered has become so corrupt that it has to be replaced by a person—someone consumed completely by zeal for the house of God.

The disciples instantly recall this reference to Psalm 69. The psalm depicts the anguish of a truly faithful person who comes into profound conflict with those whose professed concern is with the things of the spirit. The message is this: God is to be found in Jesus Christ, whose purity is inexhaustible.

The Rev. Dr. Gordon Graham
Henry Luce III Professor of Philosophy and the Arts at Princeton Theological Seminary and Priest Associate at All Saints', Princeton
Princeton, New Jersey

Questions

What are the most obvious ways in which the things of the spirit are corrupted in our day and age? What does Jesus' attack on the temple tell us about our own most treasured places?

Prayer

Almighty God, save us from the customs, conventions, and dogmas that blind. Give us the true light of faith that we may see your hand in all your works and not only in those places where we would prefer it to be. *Amen.*

DAY 6

John 3:1-15

3 Now there was a Pharisee named Nicodemus, a leader of the Jews. 2He came to Jesus by night and said to him, "Rabbi, we know that you are a teacher who has come from God; for no one can do these signs that you do apart from the presence of God." 3Jesus answered him, "Very truly, I tell you, no one can see the kingdom of God without being born from above." 4Nicodemus said to him, "How can anyone be born after having grown old? Can one enter a second time into the mother's womb and be born?" 5Jesus answered, "Very truly, I tell you, no one can enter the kingdom of God without being born of water and Spirit. 6What is born of the flesh is flesh, and what is born of the Spirit is spirit. 7Do not be astonished that I said to you, 'You must be born from above.' 8The wind blows where it chooses, and you hear the sound of it, but you do not know where it comes from or where it goes. So it is with everyone who is born of the Spirit." 9Nicodemus said to him, "How can these things be?" 10Jesus answered him, "Are you a teacher of Israel, and yet you do not understand these things?

11"Very truly, I tell you, we speak of what we know and testify to what we have seen; yet you do not receive our testimony. 12If I have told you about earthly things and you do not believe, how can you believe if I tell you about heavenly things? 13No one has ascended into heaven except the one who descended from heaven, the Son of Man. 14And just as Moses lifted up the serpent in the wilderness, so must the Son of Man be lifted up, 15that whoever believes in him may have eternal life.

Reflection

Nicodemus is a figure unique to John's Gospel; he plays the special role of a deeply sincere but indecisive spiritual seeker. He visits Jesus under the cover of darkness because consulting the itinerant preacher from Nazareth does not fit with Nicodemus's position as a prominent and respected Jewish teacher. The visit threatens to put him at odds with his fellow Pharisees. His conversation with Jesus reveals a strange mix of theological knowledge and spiritual obtuseness. We are not told exactly how it ends, but we can suppose that Nicodemus slips away as quietly as he came.

A few chapters later, he reappears, still a leading Pharisee and still someone with doubts. Nicodemus urges his more hardline colleagues to give Jesus a trial in accordance with the law, only to be accused of switching sides. In his third and final appearance, Nicodemus helps Joseph of Arimathea to take care of the body of Jesus by providing the necessary spices.

John describes Joseph as a disciple of Christ, albeit a secret one. He is never as clear about Nicodemus, who seems to remain forever torn. On the one side, Nicodemus embraces religious certainties; on the other, he perceives contrasting spiritual depths in Jesus. In Nicodemus, John the Evangelist provides us with a figure who may more accurately reflect our own relationship to Jesus than Peter, Paul, or Pilate.

The Rev. Dr. Gordon Graham
Henry Luce III Professor of Philosophy and the Arts at Princeton Theological Seminary and Priest Associate at All Saints', Princeton
Princeton, New Jersey

Questions

What matters more to you when it comes to relationships with God, community, and family: commitment or security? If you find yourself reflected in Nicodemus, does that provide hope or produce a measure of despair?

Prayer

Almighty God, you hate nothing that you have made and can see faith in indecision. Guide our faltering steps so that like Nicodemus, we may come again and again into the presence of Christ. *Amen.*

DAY 7

John 3:16-21

16“For God so loved the world
that he gave his only Son, so that
everyone who believes in him
may not perish but may have
eternal life.

17“Indeed, God did not send the
Son into the world to condemn
the world, but in order that the
world might be saved through
him. 18Those who believe in
him are not condemned; but
those who do not believe are
condemned already, because they
have not believed in the name of
the only Son of God. 19And this
is the judgment, that the light
has come into the world, and
people loved darkness rather
than light because their deeds
were evil. 20For all who do evil
hate the light and do not come to
the light, so that their deeds may
not be exposed. 21But those who
do what is true come to the light,
so that it may be clearly seen
that their deeds have been done
in God.”

Reflection

Real love is not what we think it is—it is much, much greater than our wildest, deepest imaginings. The words of John 3:16 may be known around the world, but its message is so great that it is unbelievable to many.

Whether we are aware of our own sufferings, enthralled by the horrors around us, or just numb to the world's corruption, God has a very different plan for our lives. Jesus struggles to help Nicodemus understand that the life we need comes only from himself, from the Life who has been with God from all eternity and through whom we were created. To bring us life and peace, God sends his own Life to come among us and ultimately to die on the cross to deliver us from sin and death. Jesus comes to save us from ourselves.

To believe or have faith in Jesus means to see that he is the Life of God, freely given, and to trust in him with all of our being. Faith means to see Jesus' glory and power, to recognize our own darkness, and to seek the light of his forgiveness. Faith means, finally, to dwell in Jesus, relying on his life alone, and so to have our lives changed completely. Then our character—our thoughts, words, and deeds—will indeed show what sort of people we are, on account of *whose* we are. Then all we do will reflect God's glory and beauty, and we will know what true love means.

The Rev. Dr. Christopher A. Beeley
Walter H. Gray Associate Professor of Anglican Studies and Patristics at the Berkeley Divinity School at Yale
New Haven, Connecticut

Question

How might your actions reflect darkness rather than God's light? If you do not yet know Jesus, ask him right now to turn things around in your life, then go to meet him in his Body, the Church. If you do know him, thank him for the gift of eternal life.

Prayer

O God, help us to know what real love looks like. Show us the darkness that we have chosen for our lives; help us to see the brightness of Jesus, your Son; and give us trust in his name. Thank you for the gift of Life itself. *Amen.*

DAY 8

John 3:22-36

22After this Jesus and his disciples
went into the Judean countryside,
and he spent some time there
with them and baptized. 23John
also was baptizing at Aenon
near Salim because water was
abundant there; and people kept
coming and were being baptized
24—John, of course, had not yet
been thrown into prison.

25Now a discussion about
purification arose between John's
disciples and a Jew. 26They came
to John and said to him, "Rabbi,
the one who was with you across
the Jordan, to whom you testified,
here he is baptizing, and all are
going to him." 27John answered,
"No one can receive anything
except what has been given from
heaven. 28You yourselves are my
witnesses that I said, 'I am not
the Messiah, but I have been
sent ahead of him.' 29He who has
the bride is the bridegroom. The
friend of the bridegroom, who
stands and hears him, rejoices
greatly at the bridegroom's voice.
For this reason my joy has been
fulfilled. 30He must increase, but
I must decrease."

31The one who comes from
above is above all; the one who
is of the earth belongs to the
earth and speaks about earthly
things. The one who comes from
heaven is above all. 32He testifies
to what he has seen and heard,
yet no one accepts his testimony.
33Whoever has accepted his
testimony has certified this, that
God is true. 34He whom God has
sent speaks the words of God,
for he gives the Spirit without
measure. 35The Father loves the
Son and has placed all things in
his hands. 36Whoever believes in
the Son has eternal life; whoever
disobeys the Son will not see life,
but must endure God's wrath.

Reflection

Before we meet the twelve disciples, before we are even introduced to Jesus himself, John's Gospel tells us about John the Baptist, "a man sent from God." John the Baptist is the first hero of this gospel, and here we read his last recorded words.

There is something inspiring about people who exude a sense of purpose, who know what they are about and what they need to do. John the Baptist shows that sort of commitment: he zealously follows God, and Jesus calls him the greatest person he's ever known. Of course, John is not fulfilling just any mission: He is the last of the prophets, preparing the way for the coming of Jesus, the Messiah—and John will pay for this mission with his life.

But people are worrying about who might be the greatest or who has the most followers, Jesus or John. To this nonsense John utters one of the most beautiful lines in all the gospels, his very last words: "He must increase, but I must decrease."

How difficult it is to surrender our need for glory and recognition! It is easy enough when things are going poorly: That was someone else's fault. The real challenge comes with success: Look how great we are! This is what makes John such a perfect model, not only for Christian ministers and lay leaders but also for anyone who achieves what the world considers success. May we have the character of John and give the glory, always, to God.

The Rev. Dr. Christopher A. Beeley
Walter H. Gray Associate Professor of Anglican Studies and Patristics at the Berkeley Divinity School at Yale
New Haven, Connecticut

Question

Do you have a sense of God's purpose for you at the present time? Ask God to reveal this purpose and ask for the grace always to surrender the glory to Jesus.

Prayer

Lord, we thank you for the vocations you have given us, and we ask your grace always to keep our eyes focused on Jesus. *Amen.*

DAY 9

John 4:1-42

4 Now when Jesus learned that the Pharisees had heard, "Jesus is making and baptizing more disciples than John" 2—although it was not Jesus himself but his disciples who baptized— 3he left Judea and started back to Galilee. 4But he had to go through Samaria. 5So he came to a Samaritan city called Sychar, near the plot of ground that Jacob had given to his son Joseph. 6Jacob's well was there, and Jesus, tired out by his journey, was sitting by the well. It was about noon.

7A Samaritan woman came to draw water, and Jesus said to her, "Give me a drink." 8(His disciples had gone to the city to buy food.) 9The Samaritan woman said to him, "How is it that you, a Jew, ask a drink of me, a woman of Samaria?" (Jews do not share things in common with Samaritans.) 10Jesus answered her, "If you knew the gift of God, and who it is that is saying to you, 'Give me a drink,' you would have asked him, and he would have given you living water." 11The woman said to him, "Sir, you have no bucket, and the well is deep. Where do you get that living water? 12Are you greater than our ancestor Jacob, who gave us the well, and with his sons and his flocks drank from it?" 13Jesus said to her, "Everyone who drinks of this water will be thirsty again, 14but those who drink of the water that I will give them will never be thirsty. The water that I will give will become in them a spring of water gushing up to eternal life." 15The woman said to him, "Sir, give me this water, so that I may never be thirsty or have to keep coming here to draw water."

16Jesus said to her, "Go, call your husband, and come back." 17The woman answered him, "I have

no husband." Jesus said to her,
"You are right in saying, 'I have
no husband'; 18for you have had
five husbands, and the one you
have now is not your husband.
What you have said is true!"
19The woman said to him, "Sir,
I see that you are a prophet.
20Our ancestors worshiped on
this mountain, but you say that
the place where people must
worship is in Jerusalem." 21Jesus
said to her, "Woman, believe
me, the hour is coming when
you will worship the Father
neither on this mountain nor in
Jerusalem. 22You worship what
you do not know; we worship
what we know, for salvation is
from the Jews. 23But the hour is
coming, and is now here, when
the true worshipers will worship
the Father in spirit and truth, for
the Father seeks such as these to
worship him. 24God is spirit, and
those who worship him must
worship in spirit and truth."
25The woman said to him, "I
know that Messiah is coming"
(who is called Christ). "When
he comes, he will proclaim all
things to us." 26Jesus said to her,
"I am he, the one who is speaking
to you."

27Just then his disciples came.
They were astonished that he was
speaking with a woman, but no
one said, "What do you want?"
or, "Why are you speaking with
her?" 28Then the woman left
her water jar and went back to
the city. She said to the people,
29"Come and see a man who told
me everything I have ever done!
He cannot be the Messiah, can
he?" 30They left the city and were
on their way to him.

31Meanwhile the disciples
were urging him, "Rabbi, eat
something." 32But he said to
them, "I have food to eat that
you do not know about." 33So
the disciples said to one another,
"Surely no one has brought him
something to eat?" 34Jesus said
to them, "My food is to do the
will of him who sent me and to
complete his work. 35Do you not
say, 'Four months more, then
comes the harvest'? But I tell you,
look around you, and see how

the fields are ripe for harvesting.
36The reaper is already receiving
wages and is gathering fruit for
eternal life, so that sower and
reaper may rejoice together.
37For here the saying holds true,
'One sows and another reaps.' 38I
sent you to reap that for which
you did not labor. Others have
labored, and you have entered
into their labor."

39Many Samaritans from that
city believed in him because of
the woman's testimony, "He told
me everything I have ever done."
40So when the Samaritans came
to him, they asked him to stay
with them; and he stayed there
two days. 41And many more
believed because of his word.
42They said to the woman, "It
is no longer because of what
you said that we believe, for we
have heard for ourselves, and we
know that this is truly the Savior
of the world."

Reflection

"We all know what is 'living water'," one of the Congregational churchwomen said at the 2001 conference in Majuro, the capital of the Marshall Islands. "What is important," she said, "is that Jesus knows everything about us and loves us anyway. Everything." And this is pretty much what the Samaritan woman exclaims to her townspeople, "Come and see a man who told me everything I have ever done!"

Most of these women had come to Majuro by water, some in the hold of a ship, some on outriggers, some in what looked like kayaks. Water is their island life; from water they make their living, and they know when the water has been poisoned and is dying. America's post-World War II nuclear testing in the Marshall Islands contaminated the water and has made some Marshallese exiles.

We told our stories of forgiveness and inclusion by way of the Samaritan woman at the well that summer. We celebrated Jesus' living water springing up and gushing forth and creating life after life after life. We prayed and smiled at the words, "Almighty God…from whom no secrets are hid" (*The Book of Common Prayer*, p. 355). Then, we confessed. Each of us had something to tell that we were afraid would "separate us from the love of God in Christ Jesus our Lord" (Romans 8:39).

"Even you?!" we said to each other. A liturgy emerged; we began to lift a glass of living Pacific Ocean water and thank God, who knows everything about us and loves us anyway.

The Rev. Minka S. Sprague
Director of the Chapel of the Holy Spirit,
Campus Ministry to Tulane and Loyola universities
New Orleans, Louisiana

Questions

The lifework of faith is loving ourselves and accepting God's forgiveness. What hinders us? What about our lives do we imagine shocks God? How might we let this go?

Prayer

Gracious God, guide our love of your world and our neighbors from the innermost corners of our hearts and souls. Help us find laughter and joy beyond the assurance that there is nothing we can do to lose your love. This we ask in Jesus' name. *Amen.*

DAY 10

John 4:43-54

43When the two days were
over, he went from that place
to Galilee 44(for Jesus himself
had testified that a prophet has
no honor in the prophet's own
country). 45When he came to
Galilee, the Galileans welcomed
him, since they had seen all that
he had done in Jerusalem at the
festival; for they too had gone to
the festival.

46Then he came again to Cana
in Galilee where he had changed
the water into wine. Now there
was a royal official whose son
lay ill in Capernaum. 47When he
heard that Jesus had come from
Judea to Galilee, he went and
begged him to come down and
heal his son, for he was at the
point of death. 48Then Jesus said
to him, "Unless you see signs and
wonders you will not believe."
49The official said to him, "Sir,
come down before my little boy
dies." 50Jesus said to him, "Go;
your son will live." The man
believed the word that Jesus
spoke to him and started on his
way. 51As he was going down,
his slaves met him and told him
that his child was alive. 52So he
asked them the hour when he
began to recover, and they said
to him, "Yesterday at one in the
afternoon the fever left him."
53The father realized that this
was the hour when Jesus had said
to him, "Your son will live." So
he himself believed, along with
his whole household. 54Now this
was the second sign that Jesus
did after coming from Judea to
Galilee.

Reflection

The Samaritans believe—for themselves as well as on behalf of the testimony from the woman at the well. The royal official believes, "along with his whole household," when his son recovers. When the royal official pleads for him to come to his ailing child, Jesus says, "Unless you see signs and wonders you will not believe."

The notes in my New Revised Standard Version Bible say that "you" is plural here, as if Jesus is commenting upon everyone's faith, not just the official who is afraid his son will die. Might his comment include us as well? And what about these words to Thomas: "Blessed are those who have not seen and yet have come to believe"? (20:29).

When signs and wonders are not at hand, and our lives are hard, how do we believe in the Risen Christ and in ourselves? For these times, Jesus tells us who he is throughout the Gospel; we may always look for him risen in our world. "I am," he has said—the light of the world, the bread of life, the good shepherd, the threshold, resurrection and life, the way and the truth and the life, the true vine. This is a faithful "seeing is believing," walking in the power of the Holy Spirit all our generations later in the light of the cross.

The Rev. Minka S. Sprague
Director of the Chapel of the Holy Spirit,
Campus Ministry to Tulane and Loyola universities
New Orleans, Louisiana

...tions

...s my faith the strongest? What threatens my belief in the Risen Christ? In myself? Where might I find sustenance and strength?

Prayer

Dear God, you know our ways; how easy it is to lose sight of you. Help us remember this is your world, full of love and forgiveness, a new creation. So, too, we would be. This we ask in Jesus' name, in the power of the Holy Spirit. *Amen.*

DAY 11

John 5:1-18

5 After this there was a festival of the Jews, and Jesus went up to Jerusalem.

2Now in Jerusalem by the Sheep Gate there is a pool, called in Hebrew Beth-zatha, which has five porticoes. 3In these lay many invalids—blind, lame, and paralyzed. 5One man was there who had been ill for thirty-eight years. 6When Jesus saw him lying there and knew that he had been there a long time, he said to him, "Do you want to be made well?" 7The sick man answered him, "Sir, I have no one to put me into the pool when the water is stirred up; and while I am making my way, someone else steps down ahead of me." 8Jesus said to him, "Stand up, take your mat and walk." 9At once the man was made well, and he took up his mat and began to walk. Now that day was a sabbath. 10So the Jews said to the man who had been cured, "It is the sabbath; it is not lawful for you to carry your mat." 11But he answered them, "The man who made me well said to me, 'Take up your mat and walk.'" 12They asked him, "Who is the man who said to you, 'Take it up and walk'?" 13Now the man who had been healed did not know who it was, for Jesus had disappeared in the crowd that was there. 14Later Jesus found him in the temple and said to him, "See, you have been made well! Do not sin any more, so that nothing worse happens to you." 15The man went away and told the Jews that it was Jesus who had made him well. 16Therefore the Jews started persecuting Jesus, because he was doing such things on the sabbath.

17But Jesus answered them, "My
Father is still working, and I also
am working." 18For this reason
the Jews were seeking all the
more to kill him, because he was
not only breaking the sabbath, but was also calling God his own Father, thereby making himself equal to God.

Reflection

This is not a healing story. Jesus does miraculously heal a lame man with nothing more than the command to get up, grab his mat, and walk. And yet, the healing is the catalyst for the real action.

The religious leaders are blowing a gasket. A man, who only moments before hadn't walked in nearly four decades, strolls by. You might have expected them to say, "Wow! How did that happen?" Instead, they write him a ticket for religious jaywalking: He's carrying his mat on a sabbath. Once they find out that Jesus is at the bottom of this, they throw the book at him for healing on the day of holy rest.

Breaking the sabbath law amounts to more than violating one among a long list of rules. Sabbath rest resides at the core of the religious practice of Jesus' day. Suspending the sabbath law undermines temple-centered religion.

The temple system ordered everyday life and common spiritual practice in ways that promised a relationship with and an experience of God. In Jesus, God comes to dwell in our midst in a new, more powerful way.

Religious people are rejecting Jesus on religious grounds. Clinging to their religious practices—and perhaps to the status and power that they derive from those practices—religious leaders reject God's own new way of bringing us into the divine presence. Our religious practices are good. But they are not an end in themselves. They are pathways to the holy.

The Rt. Rev. Jacob W. Owensby
Bishop of the Episcopal Diocese of Western Louisiana
Alexandria, Louisiana

Questions

Tell the story of a time that God showed up in your life in an unexpected way. How did that change your understanding of God? Of yourself?

Prayer

Gracious and holy God, who created us to participate in your holy life and to share your love with our neighbor, stretch our souls that we may receive more of you and embolden our hearts that we may love our neighbor as ourselves. In Jesus' name. *Amen.*

DAY 12

John 5:19-29

19 Jesus said to them, "Very
truly, I tell you, the Son can do
nothing on his own, but only
what he sees the Father doing;
for whatever the Father does, the
Son does likewise. 20 The Father
loves the Son and shows him
all that he himself is doing; and
he will show him greater works
than these, so that you will be
astonished. 21 Indeed, just as the
Father raises the dead and gives
them life, so also the Son gives
life to whomever he wishes.
22 The Father judges no one but
has given all judgment to the
Son, 23 so that all may honor the
Son just as they honor the Father.
Anyone who does not honor the
Son does not honor the Father
who sent him. 24 Very truly, I
tell you, anyone who hears my
word and believes him who sent
me has eternal life, and does not
come under judgment, but has
passed from death to life.

25 "Very truly, I tell you, the hour
is coming, and is now here, when
the dead will hear the voice of
the Son of God, and those who
hear will live. 26 For just as the
Father has life in himself, so
he has granted the Son also to
have life in himself; 27 and he has
given him authority to execute
judgment, because he is the Son
of Man. 28 Do not be astonished
at this; for the hour is coming
when all who are in their graves
will hear his voice 29 and will come
out—those who have done good,
to the resurrection of life, and
those who have done evil, to the
resurrection of condemnation.

Reflection

The religious authorities are up in arms. Jesus has healed on the sabbath and has called God his Father. His actions and his words suggest to them that he is claiming to be God's equal. Who does he think he is?

In response to their reaction, Jesus speaks at length about his identity. Readers of the Gospel have already heard that Jesus is the Word of God. "In the beginning...the Word was with God, and the Word was God" (1:1). Jesus is God in the flesh.

In this moment, Jesus himself speaks as a part of the gospel narrative. He tells his followers and his antagonists that he and the Father are one. But he is not arrogantly asserting equality with God like some unhinged street corner preacher. He is the obedient Son sent by the Father to do the Father's work.

The Father's work is redeeming love. Jesus is God's redeeming love in the flesh. God's love is more than a mere affection—it is the power that has brought all things into being. In Jesus, that same love is now healing and restoring the shattered creation. Jesus is God's self-revelation and God's self-giving. In Jesus, God imparts eternal life to all who believe.

The Rt. Rev. Jacob W. Owensby
Bishop of the Episcopal Diocese of Western Louisiana
Alexandria, Louisiana

Questions

Tell a story about a time that you experienced Jesus' love for you. How did that experience change your attitude toward yourself? Toward others? Toward God?

Prayer

Merciful and loving God, who became a man that we may know you and have eternal life, so transform us with your love that we may be your instruments of peace and compassion in the world. In Jesus' name. *Amen.*

DAY 13

John 5:30-47

30“I can do nothing on my
own. As I hear, I judge; and my
judgment is just, because I seek
to do not my own will but the
will of him who sent me.

31“If I testify about myself, my
testimony is not true. 32There
is another who testifies on my
behalf, and I know that his
testimony to me is true. 33You
sent messengers to John, and he
testified to the truth. 34Not that
I accept such human testimony,
but I say these things so that you
may be saved. 35He was a burning
and shining lamp, and you were
willing to rejoice for a while in
his light. 36But I have a testimony
greater than John’s. The works
that the Father has given me
to complete, the very works
that I am doing, testify on my
behalf that the Father has sent
me. 37And the Father who sent
me has himself testified on my
behalf. You have never heard his
voice or seen his form, 38and you
do not have his word abiding in
you, because you do not believe
him whom he has sent.

39“You search the scriptures
because you think that in them
you have eternal life; and it is
they that testify on my behalf.
40Yet you refuse to come to me
to have life. 41I do not accept
glory from human beings. 42But
I know that you do not have
the love of God in you. 43I have
come in my Father’s name, and
you do not accept me; if another
comes in his own name, you
will accept him. 44How can you
believe when you accept glory
from one another and do not
seek the glory that comes from
the one who alone is God? 45Do
not think that I will accuse you
before the Father; your accuser
is Moses, on whom you have
set your hope. 46If you believed
Moses, you would believe me, for
he wrote about me. 47But if you
do not believe what he wrote,
how will you believe what I say?”

Reflection

Jesus hammers away at the concept of testimony, emphasizing that his works—miracles, teachings, and indeed his entire ministry and life—are like pieces of evidence in a trial, presented to humanity to show that Jesus has been sent into the world by God.

Then Jesus reminds us—especially those of us who make a habit of regular Bible reading—of something important: that the same can be said of the scriptures. The scriptures are also testimony, or witnesses, pointing to something (some One!) beyond themselves.

Imagine a group of people gathered under a huge sign that reads, "DINING HALL: 200 YARDS→" You walk up to this group of people and say, "What are you doing here?" They say, "We're hungry, and we want to eat." You say, "Well, the Dining Hall is that way." They respond: "No, it says 'Dining Hall' right there—this must be it!"

Imagine your frustration in trying to get them to focus not on the sign but on that for which they are searching: the place to which the sign is pointing. That's the frustration Jesus must have had when he said "you search the scriptures because you think that in them you have eternal life." The scriptures *testify*—they point beyond themselves and are meant to direct people to Jesus.

In other words, our faith is not in the Bible but in the God by whom the Bible was inspired and to whom the Bible points.

The Rev. John Ohmer
Rector of The Falls Church Episcopal
Falls Church, Virginia

Questions

If the Bible testifies to God, then it could be seen as a love note from God. In what ways are you in danger of falling in love with the love note, instead of with the author of the love note? Are you in love with the author?

Prayer

God, help me to resist seeing my time of Bible study as an end in itself. Rather, help me use the scriptures as you intend them to be used: as testimony, a means to an end, pointing me toward a more loving relationship with you, my neighbor, and myself. In Jesus' name. *Amen.*

DAY 14

John 6:1-21

6 After this Jesus went to the other side of the Sea of Galilee, also called the Sea of Tiberias. 2 A large crowd kept following him, because they saw the signs that he was doing for the sick. 3 Jesus went up the mountain and sat down there with his disciples. 4 Now the Passover, the festival of the Jews, was near. 5 When he looked up and saw a large crowd coming toward him, Jesus said to Philip, "Where are we to buy bread for these people to eat?" 6 He said this to test him, for he himself knew what he was going to do. 7 Philip answered him, "Six months' wages would not buy enough bread for each of them to get a little." 8 One of his disciples, Andrew, Simon Peter's brother, said to him, 9 "There is a boy here who has five barley loaves and two fish. But what are they among so many people?" 10 Jesus said, "Make the people sit down." Now there was a great deal of grass in the place; so they sat down, about five thousand in all. 11 Then Jesus took the loaves, and when he had given thanks, he distributed them to those who were seated; so also the fish, as much as they wanted. 12 When they were satisfied, he told his disciples, "Gather up the fragments left over, so that nothing may be lost." 13 So they gathered them up, and from the fragments of the five barley loaves, left by those who had eaten, they filled twelve baskets. 14 When the people saw the sign that he had done, they began to say, "This is indeed the prophet who is to come into the world."

15 When Jesus realized that they were about to come and take him by force to make him king, he withdrew again to the mountain by himself.

16 When evening came, his disciples went down to the sea,

17 got into a boat, and started
across the sea to Capernaum.
It was now dark, and Jesus had
not yet come to them. 18 The sea
became rough because a strong
wind was blowing. 19 When they
had rowed about three or four
miles, they saw Jesus walking on
the sea and coming near the boat,
and they were terrified. 20 But
he said to them, "It is I; do not
be afraid." 21 Then they wanted
to take him into the boat, and
immediately the boat reached
the land toward which they
were going.

Reflection

Half a year's salary worth of food wouldn't be enough to feed the crowds, Jesus' followers say when asked to feed the crowds. But do you hear the faint glimmer of hope in what Andrew says next? *There is a boy here who has five barely loaves and two fish...* Five thousand hungry people is a problem that cannot be ignored and won't go away. Jesus is testing the disciples. And whenever faced with seemingly impossible odds, they have—we have—two possible reactions:

1) to stare at the problem; restate the problem; obsess about the problem, or
2) to look for "the boy."

There's always a "boy"—someone in our lives, or something deep within us, with *something* to offer, however seemingly insignificant. It is no accident that it's a boy who has the five loaves and two fish—not one of the disciples, not an adult in the crowd. A boy. A child. Recall that children were not held in high regard in first-century Palestine, so when we hear "boy," we should hear "an insignificant nobody."

There's some kid here who has five loaves and two fish...

God often acts in life—breaks into our impossible situation, helps us meet our challenge—through small, seemingly insignificant people and details (or what we so often dismiss as small, insignificant people and details). God often works miracles through the overlooked, the invisible, and the hidden.

The Rev. John Ohmer
Rector of The Falls Church Episcopal
Falls Church, Virginia

Questions

Think about a challenge you are facing. What reaction are you choosing: to restate the problem or to look for "the boy?" What small, hidden, or seemingly insignificant person or possibility are you in danger of dismissing? What might happen if you offer it to God?

Prayer

God, in your hands five loaves and two fish became abundance. When I am faced with challenges, help me remember that what I often think of as insignificant or insufficient can be, in your loving hands, the raw material of the miraculous. In Jesus' name. *Amen.*

DAY 15

John 6:22-59

22 The next day the crowd that had stayed on the other side of the sea saw that there had been only one boat there. They also saw that Jesus had not got into the boat with his disciples, but that his disciples had gone away alone. 23 Then some boats from Tiberias came near the place where they had eaten the bread after the Lord had given thanks. 24 So when the crowd saw that neither Jesus nor his disciples were there, they themselves got into the boats and went to Capernaum looking for Jesus.

25 When they found him on the other side of the sea, they said to him, “Rabbi, when did you come here?” 26 Jesus answered them, “Very truly, I tell you, you are looking for me, not because you saw signs, but because you ate your fill of the loaves. 27 Do not work for the food that perishes, but for the food that endures for eternal life, which the Son of Man will give you. For it is on him that God the Father has set his seal.”

28 Then they said to him, “What must we do to perform the works of God?” 29 Jesus answered them, “This is the work of God, that you believe in him whom he has sent.” 30 So they said to him, “What sign are you going to give us then, so that we may see it and believe you? What work are you performing? 31 Our ancestors ate the manna in the wilderness; as it is written, ‘He gave them bread from heaven to eat.’” 32 Then Jesus said to them, “Very truly, I tell you, it was not Moses who gave you the bread from heaven, but it is my Father who gives you the true bread from heaven. 33 For the bread of God is that which comes down from heaven and gives life to the world.” 34 They said to him, “Sir, give us this bread always.”

35 Jesus said to them, "I am the
bread of life. Whoever comes
to me will never be hungry, and
whoever believes in me will never
be thirsty. 36 But I said to you that
you have seen me and yet do not
believe. 37 Everything that the
Father gives me will come to me,
and anyone who comes to me I
will never drive away; 38 for I have
come down from heaven, not to
do my own will, but the will of
him who sent me. 39 And this is
the will of him who sent me, that
I should lose nothing of all that
he has given me, but raise it up
on the last day. 40 This is indeed
the will of my Father, that all
who see the Son and believe in
him may have eternal life; and
I will raise them up on the last
day."

41 Then the Jews began to
complain about him because he
said, "I am the bread that came
down from heaven." 42 They
were saying, "Is not this Jesus,
the son of Joseph, whose father
and mother we know? How can
he now say, 'I have come down
from heaven'?" 43 Jesus answered
them, "Do not complain among
yourselves. 44 No one can come to
me unless drawn by the Father
who sent me; and I will raise that
person up on the last day. 45 It
is written in the prophets, 'And
they shall all be taught by God.'
Everyone who has heard and
learned from the Father comes to
me. 46 Not that anyone has seen
the Father except the one who is
from God; he has seen the Father.
47 Very truly, I tell you, whoever
believes has eternal life. 48 I am
the bread of life. 49 Your ancestors
ate the manna in the wilderness,
and they died. 50 This is the bread
that comes down from heaven,
so that one may eat of it and
not die. 51 I am the living bread
that came down from heaven.
Whoever eats of this bread will
live forever; and the bread that I
will give for the life of the world
is my flesh."

52 The Jews then disputed among
themselves, saying, "How can
this man give us his flesh to eat?"
53 So Jesus said to them, "Very

truly, I tell you, unless you eat
the flesh of the Son of Man and
drink his blood, you have no life
in you. [54]Those who eat my flesh
and drink my blood have eternal
life, and I will raise them up on
the last day; [55]for my flesh is
true food and my blood is true
drink. [56]Those who eat my flesh
and drink my blood abide in me,
and I in them. [57]Just as the living
Father sent me, and I live because
of the Father, so whoever eats me
will live because of me. [58]This is
the bread that came down from
heaven, not like that which your
ancestors ate, and they died.
But the one who eats this bread
will live forever." [59]He said these
things while he was teaching in
the synagogue at Capernaum.

Reflection

In this lengthy and expansive discourse, John illuminates our contemporary human struggle for understanding the deep demands of faith in Jesus. Like the Jews with whom Jesus was interacting, we tend to first ask questions: "What does faith in God really require of me?" Next comes a demand for proof: "What sign will there be so I can be certain?"

As is often the case, even when the answer comes, we are still uncertain, cynical perhaps, even at times doubting the messenger. Fortunately for Christians, the answer, which Jesus provides us in this reading, is short yet has enduring and overarching power: "I am the Bread of Life." This powerful and evocative statement reminds us time and again that the selfless action of God in giving us his only Son enables us to have life in abundance on earth and in eternity. And the requirement is clear: "Whoever eats me will live because of me. This is the bread that came down from heaven."

In other words, for those who truly take in or digest Jesus inwardly into every aspect of their humanity, especially into those costly demands of true discipleship, the reward is unequivocal. "The one who eats this bread will live forever."

Dr. Jenny Te Paa-Daniel
Teacher, public theologian, social justice activist
Aitutaki, Cook Islands

Questions

Do you ask questions of God, demanding a sign or even doubting God's promises? How does reconsidering this gospel reading help you to understand your hesitancy and uncertainty?

Prayer

God of love, we give you thanks for your flesh and blood poured out so freely in order that we might have life eternal in you. Help us each day to be less questioning, less demanding, less doubting of what it means to truly eat this bread and live forever. *Amen.*

DAY 16

John 6:60-71

[60]When many of his disciples heard it, they said, "This teaching is difficult; who can accept it?" [61]But Jesus, being aware that his disciples were complaining about it, said to them, "Does this offend you? [62]Then what if you were to see the Son of Man ascending to where he was before? [63]It is the spirit that gives life; the flesh is useless. The words that I have spoken to you are spirit and life. [64]But among you there are some who do not believe." For Jesus knew from the first who were the ones that did not believe, and who was the one that would betray him. [65]And he said, "For this reason I have told you that no one can come to me unless it is granted by the Father."

[66]Because of this many of his disciples turned back and no longer went about with him. [67]So Jesus asked the twelve, "Do you also wish to go away?" [68]Simon Peter answered him, "Lord, to whom can we go? You have the words of eternal life. [69]We have come to believe and know that you are the Holy One of God." [70]Jesus answered them, "Did I not choose you, the twelve? Yet one of you is a devil." [71]He was speaking of Judas son of Simon Iscariot, for he, though one of the twelve, was going to betray him.

Reflection

Just like the disciples, we often find the teachings of Jesus hard to accept. Theologian William Barclay reminds us, "Time and again, it is not the intellectual difficulty which keeps us from being good Christians; it is the height of Christ's moral demand."

As John so poignantly describes in this gospel passage, the situation for Jesus is changing dramatically. The crowds are now less numerous and far less certain. The cross is looming, and it is here, at the point of danger, when holding to the moral high ground becomes so risky that many of the disciples opt out, or worse, choose duplicity.

It is precisely at points such as this that the example of Simon Peter is so profound. In this moment at least, his is a faith based not on intellectual understandings but on a personal relationship with Jesus. Peter's allegiance to Jesus is not philosophically or even theoretically based; rather he gives his absolute allegiance and unequivocal love because his heart will not allow him to do any less. No wonder he can say to Jesus with such unblemished faith, "You have the words of eternal life. We have come to believe and know that you are the Holy One of God."

Dr. Jenny Te Paa-Daniel
Teacher, public theologian, social justice activist
Aitutaki, Cook Islands

Questions

Think of the times when you have grappled with the moral demands of Christian faith. Have you wavered in taking a moral stance on an issue that could leave you exposed and unpopular? What were the consequences?

Prayer

God of mercy, help us always to be fearless in our faith and able to maintain ourselves in right relationship with you. Help us always to receive with grace and courage the words of eternal life gifted to us by the Holy One of God. *Amen.*

DAY 17

John 7:1-31

7 After this Jesus went about in Galilee. He did not wish to go about in Judea because the Jews were looking for an opportunity to kill him. 2Now the Jewish festival of Booths was near. 3So his brothers said to him, "Leave here and go to Judea so that your disciples also may see the works you are doing; 4for no one who wants to be widely known acts in secret. If you do these things, show yourself to the world." 5(For not even his brothers believed in him.) 6Jesus said to them, "My time has not yet come, but your time is always here. 7The world cannot hate you, but it hates me because I testify against it that its works are evil. 8Go to the festival yourselves. I am not going to this festival, for my time has not yet fully come." 9After saying this, he remained in Galilee.

10But after his brothers had gone to the festival, then he also went, not publicly but as it were in secret. 11The Jews were looking for him at the festival and saying, "Where is he?" 12And there was considerable complaining about him among the crowds. While some were saying, "He is a good man," others were saying, "No, he is deceiving the crowd." 13Yet no one would speak openly about him for fear of the Jews.

14About the middle of the festival Jesus went up into the temple and began to teach. 15The Jews were astonished at it, saying, "How does this man have such learning, when he has never been taught?" 16Then Jesus answered them, "My teaching is not mine but his who sent me. 17Anyone who resolves to do the will of God will know whether the teaching is from God or whether I am speaking on my own. 18Those who speak on their own seek their own glory; but the one who seeks the glory of him

who sent him is true, and there is
nothing false in him.

19“Did not Moses give you the
law? Yet none of you keeps the
law. Why are you looking for an
opportunity to kill me?” 20The
crowd answered, “You have a
demon! Who is trying to kill
you?” 21Jesus answered them, “I
performed one work, and all of
you are astonished. 22Moses gave
you circumcision (it is, of course,
not from Moses, but from the
patriarchs), and you circumcise a
man on the sabbath. 23If a man
receives circumcision on the
sabbath in order that the law of
Moses may not be broken, are
you angry with me because I
healed a man’s whole body on
the sabbath? 24Do not judge by
appearances, but judge with
right judgment.”

25Now some of the people of
Jerusalem were saying, “Is not
this the man whom they are
trying to kill? 26And here he is,
speaking openly, but they say
nothing to him! Can it be that
the authorities really know that
this is the Messiah? 27Yet we
know where this man is from;
but when the Messiah comes, no
one will know where he is from.”
28Then Jesus cried out as he was
teaching in the temple, “You
know me, and you know where I
am from. I have not come on my
own. But the one who sent me is
true, and you do not know him.
29I know him, because I am from
him, and he sent me.” 30Then
they tried to arrest him, but no
one laid hands on him, because
his hour had not yet come. 31Yet
many in the crowd believed in
him and were saying, “When the
Messiah comes, will he do more
signs than this man has done?”

Reflection

Having seen and heard Jesus, what do those who observe him closely really think? The doctors of the law and the scribes, it seems, have a hunch. But Jesus disturbs and challenges the comforts and certainties of the religion of his day. He invites us to contemplate the difference between knowing *about* God and actually knowing God *personally*.

Nearly everyone had an opinion about Jesus—as nearly everyone does today. But the question, "Is not this the man whom they are trying to kill?"—essentially, "Is this the Christ?"—is really another way of asking, "If that's what you think, what are you going to do about it? What difference will it make to you?" The questions expose Jesus' critics—the gap between rhetoric and reality, between knowledge and faith. The critics of Jesus know that he is significant, but they do little about it.

The moment we respond to the question, "Is this the Christ?", with an emphatic yes, we know the answer is going to cost us. For the moment the words are uttered, there can be no going back. We cannot follow Jesus as one might follow a favorite TV program or baseball team. Following Jesus requires a total reordering of life.

Christianity is not a consumer lifestyle with options of multiple-choice questions. Discipleship is, in essence, the simply uttered word yes. This is a yes to God, the letting go of life and embracing of a new future.

The Very Rev. Dr. Martyn Percy
Dean of Christ Church, Oxford and the
Cathedral Church of the Diocese of Oxford
Oxford, England

Questions

Looking back, how has responding to Jesus changed your life? What in your life still needs challenging and converting?

Prayer

Lord Jesus, you call us to set ourselves aside and follow you. You invite us to join in your work of conversion and transformation. In your mission to convict, challenge, and change this world that you love, begin your work in our lives, so we may be continually converted. *Amen.*

DAY 18

John 7:32-53; 8:1

32The Pharisees heard the crowd muttering such things about him, and the chief priests and Pharisees sent temple police to arrest him. 33Jesus then said, "I will be with you a little while longer, and then I am going to him who sent me. 34You will search for me, but you will not find me; and where I am, you cannot come." 35The Jews said to one another, "Where does this man intend to go that we will not find him? Does he intend to go to the Dispersion among the Greeks and teach the Greeks? 36What does he mean by saying, 'You will search for me and you will not find me' and 'Where I am, you cannot come'?"

37On the last day of the festival, the great day, while Jesus was standing there, he cried out, "Let anyone who is thirsty come to me, 38and let the one who believes in me drink. As the scripture has said, 'Out of the believer's heart shall flow rivers of living water.'" 39Now he said this about the Spirit, which believers in him were to receive; for as yet there was no Spirit, because Jesus was not yet glorified.

40When they heard these words, some in the crowd said, "This is really the prophet." 41Others said, "This is the Messiah." But some asked, "Surely the Messiah does not come from Galilee, does he? 42Has not the scripture said that the Messiah is descended from David and comes from Bethlehem, the village where David lived?" 43So there was a division in the crowd because of him. 44Some of them wanted to arrest him, but no one laid hands on him.

45Then the temple police went back to the chief priests and Pharisees, who asked them, "Why did you not arrest him?" 46The police answered, "Never

has anyone spoken like this!"
47Then the Pharisees replied,
"Surely you have not been
deceived too, have you? 48Has any
one of the authorities or of the
Pharisees believed in him? 49But
this crowd, which does not know
the law—they are accursed."
50Nicodemus, who had gone to
Jesus before, and who was one of
them, asked, 51"Our law does not
judge people without first giving
them a hearing to find out what
they are doing, does it?" 52They
replied, "Surely you are not also
from Galilee, are you? Search
and you will see that no prophet
is to arise from Galilee." 53Then
each of them went home,

8 while Jesus went to the
Mount of Olives.

Reflection

There is a world of difference between dead water and living water. Water that is dead calm can be fine—safe to swim in and peaceful. But sometimes dead calm water is just that—dead. And you can't be calmer than dead. Except dead water often teems with life— usually the wrong kind, with impurities, parasites, and disease. Unless the water comes from a safe, deep well, the wisest thing is to drink from a flowing river or spring. The water is always fresh and rich in minerals. It flows fast and pure.

Jesus knows perfectly well that his audience understands the value of wells and rivers. They know about the dangers of dead pools of water and give a wide berth to them. So, from where does this living water flow?

Earlier we read about Jesus talking to a Samaritan woman at a well: "Everyone who drinks of this water will be thirsty again, but those who drink of the water that I will give them will never be thirsty. The water that I will give will become in them a spring of water gushing up to eternal life." The living water that flows as promised by Jesus is life-giving, and he is also the source of it. Like the water that flows from Jesus' side on the cross, we are to understand the water of life—deep wells and flowing rivers—as being sourced from God.

We are thirsty and invited to drink; we are filthy and invited to wash; we are weary and invited to be refreshed. God's river of life-giving water now flows to us all—just as God's grace, mercy, peace, and love are poured out abundantly upon us.

The Very Rev. Dr. Martyn Percy
Dean of Christ Church, Oxford and the
Cathedral Church of the Diocese of Oxford
Oxford, England

Questions

How does the river of life flow through us? What does it bring to us, and what does it wash away?

Prayer

Gracious God, source of life-giving water, wash away our sins, refresh our weary souls, quench our dry hearts, and renew our thirsty minds. Inspire us with your life-giving water, which alone can redeem, renew, and replenish, so we may be refreshed in our love and service to one another, and for you. *Amen.*

DAY 19

John 8:2-20

2 Early in the morning he came
again to the temple. All the
people came to him and he sat
down and began to teach them.
3 The scribes and the Pharisees
brought a woman who had been
caught in adultery; and making
her stand before all of them,
4 they said to him, "Teacher, this
woman was caught in the very act
of committing adultery. 5 Now in
the law Moses commanded us to
stone such women. Now what
do you say?" 6 They said this to
test him, so that they might have
some charge to bring against
him. Jesus bent down and wrote
with his finger on the ground.
7 When they kept on questioning
him, he straightened up and said
to them, "Let anyone among you
who is without sin be the first
to throw a stone at her." 8 And
once again he bent down and
wrote on the ground. 9 When
they heard it, they went away,
one by one, beginning with the
elders; and Jesus was left alone
with the woman standing before
him. 10 Jesus straightened up and
said to her, "Woman, where are
they? Has no one condemned
you?" 11 She said, "No one, sir."
And Jesus said, "Neither do I
condemn you. Go your way, and
from now on do not sin again."

12 Again Jesus spoke to them,
saying, "I am the light of the
world. Whoever follows me will
never walk in darkness but will
have the light of life." 13 Then
the Pharisees said to him, "You
are testifying on your own
behalf; your testimony is not
valid." 14 Jesus answered, "Even
if I testify on my own behalf,
my testimony is valid because I
know where I have come from
and where I am going, but you
do not know where I come from
or where I am going. 15 You judge
by human standards; I judge no

one. 16Yet even if I do judge, my judgment is valid; for it is not I alone who judge, but I and the Father who sent me. 17In your law it is written that the testimony of two witnesses is valid. 18I testify on my own behalf, and the Father who sent me testifies on my behalf." 19Then they said to him, "Where is your Father?" Jesus answered, "You know neither me nor my Father. If you knew me, you would know my Father also." 20He spoke these words while he was teaching in the treasury of the temple, but no one arrested him, because his hour had not yet come.

Reflection

This woman stands before Jesus, her soul and body trembling. Caught with a man other than her husband, she faces imminent death. We will never know the details: if she willingly seduced someone, if this was a moment of love in an otherwise harsh life, or if she is the victim of sexual violence.

But we do know, as does she, that the punishment in her community for stepping outside marriage is stoning. No wonder she doesn't say anything: She must be terrified.

Yet unlike the men who have dragged her to the temple, Jesus is silent.

Surprisingly, he crouches down and writes in the dirt. And then he stands, saying to her accusers: *Go ahead. Throw your stones. Whoever is without sin should throw the first one.*

One by one, the men go away. The woman is alone with Jesus.

Jesus: "Woman, where are they [who accused you]? Has no one condemned you?"

The woman (and this is the shortest word count on record for any woman who speaks in the Bible): "No one, sir."

Jesus: "Neither do I condemn you. Go your way, and from now on do not sin again."

Our Lord is about healing and forgiveness, about setting the other free. May we learn from this encounter about not being the ones who drag others before God, expecting harsh punishment for them, but about being God's people who listen, heal, and help the accused find another way home.

The Rev. Lindsay Hardin Freeman
Episcopal priest, author, and adjunct clergy at St. David's Church
Minnetonka, Minnesota

Questions

What does this mean for us when we are quick to judge and assign blame to others? What does Jesus want us to think about before we say words that we might not be able to take back?

Prayer

Dear Lord, we don't know what you were writing in the dirt that day, but you took the time to think about things and so should we. We have all sinned; we have all fallen short. We have judged others when we haven't known the whole truth or what springs from another's heart. Help us, Lord, to be more like you. Help us make amends on your behalf, forgive others in your name, and find joy where we have been numbed by pain. All this we ask in your name. *Amen.*

DAY 20

John 8:21-38

21 Again he said to them, "I am
going away, and you will search
for me, but you will die in your
sin. Where I am going, you
cannot come." 22 Then the Jews
said, "Is he going to kill himself?
Is that what he means by saying,
'Where I am going, you cannot
come'?" 23 He said to them, "You
are from below, I am from above;
you are of this world, I am not of
this world. 24 I told you that you
would die in your sins, for you
will die in your sins unless you
believe that I am he." 25 They said
to him, "Who are you?" Jesus said
to them, "Why do I speak to you
at all? 26 I have much to say about
you and much to condemn; but
the one who sent me is true, and
I declare to the world what I have
heard from him." 27 They did not
understand that he was speaking
to them about the Father. 28 So
Jesus said, "When you have
lifted up the Son of Man, then
you will realize that I am he, and
that I do nothing on my own,
but I speak these things as the
Father instructed me. 29 And the
one who sent me is with me; he
has not left me alone, for I always
do what is pleasing to him." 30 As
he was saying these things, many
believed in him.

31 Then Jesus said to the Jews
who had believed in him, "If
you continue in my word, you
are truly my disciples; 32 and
you will know the truth, and
the truth will make you free."
33 They answered him, "We are
descendants of Abraham and
have never been slaves to anyone.
What do you mean by saying,
'You will be made free'?" 34 Jesus
answered them, "Very truly, I
tell you, everyone who commits
sin is a slave to sin. 35 The slave

does not have a permanent place
in the household; the son has a
place there forever. 36So if the
Son makes you free, you will be
free indeed. 37I know that you
are descendants of Abraham; yet
you look for an opportunity to
kill me, because there is no place
in you for my word.

38I declare what I have seen in the
Father's presence; as for you, you
should do what you have heard
from the Father."

Reflection

The first word in today's passage is "again." How often that word occurs in John's Gospel—where Jesus has to explain things, over and over, for a listening audience that just does not understand.

We can sense Jesus' frustration. *Why do I bother? Will these people ever understand what I'm doing...what I'm trying to do? Of course they do not understand where I'm about to go—because they don't know who I am, nor do they grasp everything I've said, everything I've done, everyone I've loved.*

Even Jesus grew frustrated in his ministry. Even he got tired. Even he was tempted. Yet he did not give up but gave his all.

Writer Annie Dillard once said: "One of the few things I know about writing is this: Spend it all, shoot it, play it, lose it, all, right away, every time." The same could be said of living in the world as a Christian. Jesus would not have us give up. Jesus would not have us try to spread his Word only half-heartedly.

Such an approach does not mean working 24/7, for even God rested on the seventh day, and Jesus sought out plenty of quiet places. But he kept trying. Sometimes Jesus had to say the same things over and over, prefacing them with "again," as he does in today's reading.

We take our cue from him. We keep going. We keep trying. He asks us for no less.

The Rev. Lindsay Hardin Freeman
Episcopal priest, author, and adjunct clergy at St. David's Church
Minnetonka, Minnesota

Questions

If you are feeling fractured, what priority in your life would Jesus have you attend to first? Second? What burdens might God encourage you to set down?

Even God rested from the work of creation, and Jesus sought out quiet places to recharge. What times of rest and reflection are built into your schedule today?

Prayer

Lord, I give you those burdens in my heart today that are weighing me down. I ask for your intervention, your joy, and your Spirit. Bless those for whom I can pray no longer. Watch over them and keep them safe in your loving arms. And bless those who have traveled with me, that we may continue to stay close. All this I ask in your name. *Amen.*

DAY 21

John 8:39-59

39They answered him, "Abraham
is our father." Jesus said to them,
"If you were Abraham's children,
you would be doing what
Abraham did, 40but now you are
trying to kill me, a man who has
told you the truth that I heard
from God. This is not what
Abraham did. 41You are indeed
doing what your father does."
They said to him, "We are not
illegitimate children; we have
one father, God himself." 42Jesus
said to them, "If God were your
Father, you would love me, for I
came from God and now I am
here. I did not come on my own,
but he sent me. 43Why do you
not understand what I say? It is
because you cannot accept my
word. 44You are from your father
the devil, and you choose to do
your father's desires. He was a
murderer from the beginning
and does not stand in the truth,
because there is no truth in
him. When he lies, he speaks
according to his own nature, for
he is a liar and the father of lies.
45But because I tell the truth, you
do not believe me. 46Which of
you convicts me of sin? If I tell
the truth, why do you not believe
me? 47Whoever is from God
hears the words of God. The
reason you do not hear them is
that you are not from God."

48The Jews answered him, "Are
we not right in saying that you
are a Samaritan and have a
demon?" 49Jesus answered, "I do
not have a demon; but I honor
my Father, and you dishonor me.
50Yet I do not seek my own glory;
there is one who seeks it and he
is the judge. 51Very truly, I tell
you, whoever keeps my word will
never see death." 52The Jews said
to him, "Now we know that you
have a demon. Abraham died,
and so did the prophets; yet you
say, 'Whoever keeps my word
will never taste death.' 53Are you

greater than our father Abraham,
who died? The prophets also
died. Who do you claim to be?”
54Jesus answered, “If I glorify
myself, my glory is nothing. It is
my Father who glorifies me, he of
whom you say, ‘He is our God,’
55though you do not know him.
But I know him; if I would say
that I do not know him, I would
be a liar like you. But I do know
him and I keep his word. 56Your
ancestor Abraham rejoiced that
he would see my day; he saw it
and was glad.” 57Then the Jews
said to him, “You are not yet
fifty years old, and have you seen
Abraham?” 58Jesus said to them,
“Very truly, I tell you, before
Abraham was, I am.” 59So they
picked up stones to throw at
him, but Jesus hid himself and
went out of the temple.

Reflection

Many believers think about their Christian faith and practice as *either* a faith *or* a practice—something to be believed or something to be done. In reality, Christianity is *both* a faith *and* a practice. We must believe what is right (orthodoxy) and put that belief into action (orthopraxy). Many of us want to settle for one or the other rather than integrating both into our lives of faith. We hope that our belief in the Lord Jesus will cover a multitude of the minor sins that we commit each day. Or, we think that if we do good in the world, God will forgive our lack of trust.

But we must trust *and* act. We must trust that God—the God of all time who is present now with Jesus, Abraham, and all of us— wills what is best for us and that ultimately God's will shall be accomplished. We must act in accordance with that trust in our actions, which will make God's redeeming love known to the world. If not, we cease to be agents of God's kingdom and become servants of another will—one in opposition to God.

To know God's timeless will, we must seek to know God as revealed in scripture, history, and especially in the acts of redemptive love shown in the life and ministry of Jesus. That is the will, the way, the shape of our Christian faith—a way that leads not to its own glory, but God's. Not its own will, but God's.

The Rev. Gideon L. K. Pollach
Rector of St. John's Church
Cold Spring Harbor, New York

Questions

How does your life of faith reveal God's will and glory? How has your practice of faith been inspired by your trust that God's will shall be done?

Prayer

O God of all time, every moment of time is present to you. Inspire us to be agents of your kingdom on earth now as it is in heaven. Give us wisdom always to believe and do what is right so that our lives may be signs of your glory. *Amen.*

DAY 22

John 9:1-12

9 As he walked along, he saw a man blind from birth. 2His disciples asked him, "Rabbi, who sinned, this man or his parents, that he was born blind?" 3Jesus answered, "Neither this man nor his parents sinned; he was born blind so that God's works might be revealed in him. 4We must work the works of him who sent me while it is day; night is coming when no one can work. 5As long as I am in the world, I am the light of the world." 6When he had said this, he spat on the ground and made mud with the saliva and spread the mud on the man's eyes, 7saying to him, "Go, wash in the pool of Siloam" (which means Sent). Then he went and washed and came back able to see.

8The neighbors and those who had seen him before as a beggar began to ask, "Is this not the man who used to sit and beg?" 9Some were saying, "It is he." Others were saying, "No, but it is someone like him." He kept saying, "I am the man." 10But they kept asking him, "Then how were your eyes opened?" 11He answered, "The man called Jesus made mud, spread it on my eyes, and said to me, 'Go to Siloam and wash.' Then I went and washed and received my sight." 12They said to him, "Where is he?" He said, "I do not know."

Reflection

One of the most popular hashtags on Twitter is #blessed. It is used in that sphere to suggest that the many good things that happen to us over the course of our day are signs of God's favor. Similarly, and conversely, it speaks also to an ancient mindset that believes misfortunes are signs of God's condemnation of our lives. We see this in scripture in the interpretation of Israel's successes and failures in the book of Judges. We also see it in this passage from John.

Ancient minds believed that illness was a sign of human sinfulness. This belief is behind the disciples' question about the blind man. The idea may lurk deep in your heart also—especially in moments of weakness, illness, or struggle.

Truthfully, all of us sin, all of us are blessed, and all of us can be vehicles for the display of God's glory working in us. Nothing needs to stand in the way of God's will being accomplished through us. It is through mud made with saliva that Jesus reveals the great redemptive love of God, and it is through our weak hands that God is able to make God's work known.

The Rev. Gideon L. K. Pollach
Rector of St. John's Church
Cold Spring Harbor, New York

Questions

How can you know and experience the depth of God's blessing in the midst of your everyday suffering? How can rethinking the nature of God's blessing be a source of grace in your life?

Prayer

Gracious Lord, save us from simplistic thinking. Help us to see and know that in the strains and stresses of our lives, you are blessing in equal measure. Help us to accept and endure all that confronts us in each day, and may your grace abide with us always. *Amen.*

DAY 23

John 9:13-41

13They brought to the Pharisees the man who had formerly been blind. 14Now it was a sabbath day when Jesus made the mud and opened his eyes. 15Then the Pharisees also began to ask him how he had received his sight. He said to them, “He put mud on my eyes. Then I washed, and now I see.” 16Some of the Pharisees said, “This man is not from God, for he does not observe the sabbath.” But others said, “How can a man who is a sinner perform such signs?” And they were divided. 17So they said again to the blind man, “What do you say about him? It was your eyes he opened.” He said, “He is a prophet.”

18The Jews did not believe that he had been blind and had received his sight until they called the parents of the man who had received his sight 19and asked them, “Is this your son, who you say was born blind? How then does he now see?” 20His parents answered, “We know that this is our son, and that he was born blind; 21but we do not know how it is that now he sees, nor do we know who opened his eyes. Ask him; he is of age. He will speak for himself.” 22His parents said this because they were afraid of the Jews; for the Jews had already agreed that anyone who confessed Jesus to be the Messiah would be put out of the synagogue. 23Therefore his parents said, “He is of age; ask him.”

24So for the second time they called the man who had been blind, and they said to him, “Give glory to God! We know that this man is a sinner.” 25He answered, “I do not know whether he is a sinner. One thing I do know, that though I was blind, now I see.” 26They said to him, "What did he do to you? How did he open your eyes?" [27]He answered them, "I have told you already, and you would not listen. Why do you want to hear it again? Do you also want to become his disciples?" [28]Then they reviled him, saying, "You are his disciple, but we are disciples of Moses. [29]We know that God has spoken to Moses, but as for this man, we do not know where he comes from." [30]The man answered, "Here is an astonishing thing! You do not know where he comes from, and yet he opened my eyes. [31]We know that God does not listen to sinners, but he does listen to one who worships him and obeys his will. [32]Never since the world began has it been heard that anyone opened the eyes of a person born blind. [33]If this man were not from God, he could do nothing." [34]They answered him, "You were born entirely in sins, and are you trying to teach us?" And they drove him out.

[35]Jesus heard that they had driven him out, and when he found him, he said, "Do you believe in the Son of Man?" [36]He answered, "And who is he, sir? Tell me, so that I may believe in him." [37]Jesus said to him, "You have seen him, and the one speaking with you is he." [38]He said, "Lord, I believe." And he worshiped him.

[39]Jesus said, "I came into this world for judgment so that those who do not see may see, and those who do see may become blind." [40]Some of the Pharisees near him heard this and said to him, "Surely we are not blind, are we?" [41]Jesus said to them, "If you were blind, you would not have sin. But now that you say, 'We see,' your sin remains."

Reflection

After the blind man washes his eyes, we see him through the eyes of people who can no longer make sense of him. For neighbors, religious leaders, and family members, the man becomes a violation of their most basic understanding about how things work.

We hear the man's voice begin to emerge with strength, clarity, and conviction. When relentlessly peppered with questions and accusations, this unnamed man answers simply and directly. Jesus "put mud on my eyes. Then I washed, and now I see."

God's transforming grace in one person overflows and opens possibilities for even more change. But we humans, alone and in groups, have well-rehearsed barriers and blind spots. We can become like the Pharisees, hell-bent on keeping ourselves and others in conformity to rehearsed scripts.

And yet the healing power of God will not conform or retreat. The cat is out of the bag. Jesus has made mud and healed on the sabbath, violating our standards—and now, someone born blind can see. The Pharisees cannot deny what is right in front of them without denying reality, driving out the one who now sees and speaks with passionate clarity.

Jesus does not leave this unnamed one abandoned. The last veil is lifted, and he sees Jesus.

The Rev. Dr. David T. Gortner
Associate Dean of Church and Community Engagement
at Virginia Theological Seminary
Alexandria, Virginia

Questions

Who are you in this story? For whom have you opened doors? For whom have you shut doors? What are your simple and direct words that express what God has done in your life?

Prayer

Holy Spirit, open my eyes and heart to seek and see Jesus in others' lives, to embrace and celebrate more of God's surprising violations. Lord, free me from my own willful blindness. And open my mouth and my will to speak that I may be as clear and direct in my speech as this one transformed by Jesus. *Amen.*

DAY 24

John 10:1-21

10 “Very truly, I tell you, anyone who does not enter the sheepfold by the gate but climbs in by another way is a thief and a bandit. 2The one who enters by the gate is the shepherd of the sheep. 3The gatekeeper opens the gate for him, and the sheep hear his voice. He calls his own sheep by name and leads them out. 4When he has brought out all his own, he goes ahead of them, and the sheep follow him because they know his voice. 5They will not follow a stranger, but they will run from him because they do not know the voice of strangers.” 6Jesus used this figure of speech with them, but they did not understand what he was saying to them.

7So again Jesus said to them, “Very truly, I tell you, I am the gate for the sheep. 8All who came before me are thieves and bandits; but the sheep did not listen to them. 9I am the gate. Whoever enters by me will be saved, and will come in and go out and find pasture. 10The thief comes only to steal and kill and destroy. I came that they may have life, and have it abundantly.

11“I am the good shepherd. The good shepherd lays down his life for the sheep. 12The hired hand, who is not the shepherd and does not own the sheep, sees the wolf coming and leaves the sheep and runs away—and the wolf snatches them and scatters them. 13The hired hand runs away because a hired hand does not care for the sheep. 14I am the good shepherd. I know my own and my own know me, 15just as the Father knows me and I know the Father. And I lay down my life for the sheep. 16I have other sheep that do not belong to this fold. I must bring them also, and they will listen to my voice. So there will be one flock, one shepherd. [17]For this reason the Father loves me, because I lay down my life in order to take it up again. [18]No one takes it from me, but I lay it down of my own accord. I have power to lay it down, and I have power to take it up again. I have received this command from my Father."

[19]Again the Jews were divided because of these words. [20]Many of them were saying, "He has a demon and is out of his mind. Why listen to him?" [21]Others were saying, "These are not the words of one who has a demon. Can a demon open the eyes of the blind?"

Reflection

On one hand, trust. On the other hand, fear and suspicion.

I remember old movies of goslings following biologist Konrad Lorenz everywhere, all through their adolescence. The young geese had "imprinted" on Lorenz as the first moving thing they encountered after opening their eyes. Automatic imprinting is a rudimentary form of trust, hardwired into some animals' neural systems to prepare them to jump up and follow their parents. But what if their parents are not the first thing they see? Lorenz became the parent the goslings needed. He helped them become geese—even wading into the water so that they would learn to swim.

As children develop strong attachment to the ones who give them love and care, they also develop deep uncertainty around new people (stranger anxiety). This response is self-protective and helps them learn not to give their trust away too freely. Trust is given when someone earns their trust, and their parents become the gateways and checkpoints for opening up to new people and situations.

Jesus is the One we most deeply and truly recognize: *My sheep know my voice and trust me.* We sense that we can trust this voice, this presence, because we know it is deeply familiar. It is as if we have heard this voice and felt this presence all our lives. We have been wired to recognize the song of love—we sheep of *any* fold, from any place and time and situation. This is no stranger without history. This is no thief, trying to take advantage of us. It is God-with-us, Emmanuel, the One who has been with us all along from the beginning.

The Rev. Dr. David T. Gortner
Associate Dean of Church and Community Engagement
at Virginia Theological Seminary
Alexandria, Virginia

Questions

When have you heard the voice of the One who knows you most deeply, who you knew you could trust completely? When have you given yourself fully to others who have invested care and trust in you?

Prayer

Shepherd of us all, thank you. You are that presence that I know and trust. You are that voice that I recognize more deeply than any other. You are the safe place. I trust you to walk with me and to be my gateway. As it is for me, so it is for every one of us that you love. I am so grateful. Let me rest in the trust of your care. *Amen.*

Day 25

John 10:22-42

22At that time the festival of
the Dedication took place in
Jerusalem. It was winter, 23and
Jesus was walking in the temple,
in the portico of Solomon. 24So
the Jews gathered around him
and said to him, "How long will
you keep us in suspense? If you
are the Messiah, tell us plainly."
25Jesus answered, "I have told
you, and you do not believe. The
works that I do in my Father's
name testify to me; 26but you do
not believe, because you do not
belong to my sheep. 27My sheep
hear my voice. I know them, and
they follow me. 28I give them
eternal life, and they will never
perish. No one will snatch them
out of my hand. 29What my
Father has given me is greater
than all else, and no one can
snatch it out of the Father's hand.
30The Father and I are one."

31The Jews took up stones again
to stone him. 32Jesus replied,
"I have shown you many good
works from the Father. For
which of these are you going to
stone me?" 33The Jews answered,
"It is not for a good work that we
are going to stone you, but for
blasphemy, because you, though
only a human being, are making
yourself God." 34Jesus answered,
"Is it not written in your law, 'I
said, you are gods'? 35If those to
whom the word of God came
were called 'gods' —and the
scripture cannot be annulled—
36can you say that the one whom
the Father has sanctified and sent
into the world is blaspheming
because I said, 'I am God's Son'?
37If I am not doing the works of
my Father, then do not believe
me. 38But if I do them, even
though you do not believe me,
believe the works, so that you
may know and understand that
the Father is in me and I am in
the Father."

[39]Then they tried to arrest him
again, but he escaped from their
hands.

[40]He went away again across the
Jordan to the place where John
had been baptizing earlier, and
he remained there. [41]Many came
to him, and they were saying,
"John performed no sign, but
everything that John said about
this man was true." [42]And many
believed in him there.

Reflection

The most painful rifts can be within families, as you may know from your own experiences. No one can hurt you as badly as someone who knows you well, and when you share many things with someone else, the differences can stand out all the more powerfully. That is why it's so important to read the Gospel of John's many references to "the Jews" not as arguments between Jesus and a set of enemies but as disagreements within an extended family.

Jesus was a Jew, of course, as were the disciples who gathered around him, so to think of "the Jews" as some monolithic force opposing the kingdom of God—an interpretation that has led to centuries of anti-Semitism—is to badly misread the story. Some scholars think these biting references to "the Jews" actually reflect the situation of the early Christian community for whom the Gospel of John was their normative text. Perhaps they had been excluded from the synagogue and the Jewish community because of their belief that Jesus was the Messiah. Imagine how painful that rejection would have felt!

It may help to imagine these as conversations between faithful people seeking how best to serve God. "The Jews" ask Jesus to prove who he is because they too are seeking the Anointed One who will usher in a new era for God's Chosen. Sadly, like others in the gospels, many do not see that Jesus is that one. Happily, there are others who hear Jesus' voice, recognize him as their shepherd, and follow.

Dr. Greg Garrett
Professor of English at Baylor University
Writer in Residence at the Seminary of the Southwest
Austin, Texas

Questions

When have you experienced disagreement within your faith community? How have those disagreements been resolved? What brokenness still needs to be mended in the life of your family, your church, and your community?

Prayer

Holy One of Blessing, you have given us the ministry of reconciliation. Help us to see all members of the human family not only as your beloved children but also as companions who seek your face, for the sake of him who reconciled us to you, your Son, our Savior, Jesus Christ. *Amen.*

Day 26

John 11:1-44

11 Now a certain man was
ill, Lazarus of Bethany,
the village of Mary and her sister
Martha. 2Mary was the one who
anointed the Lord with perfume
and wiped his feet with her hair;
her brother Lazarus was ill. 3So
the sisters sent a message to
Jesus, "Lord, he whom you love
is ill." 4But when Jesus heard it,
he said, "This illness does not
lead to death; rather it is for
God's glory, so that the Son of
God may be glorified through
it." 5Accordingly, though Jesus
loved Martha and her sister and
Lazarus, 6after having heard that
Lazarus was ill, he stayed two
days longer in the place where he
was.

7Then after this he said to the
disciples, "Let us go to Judea
again." 8The disciples said to
him, "Rabbi, the Jews were just
now trying to stone you, and
are you going there again?"
9Jesus answered, "Are there
not twelve hours of daylight?
Those who walk during the
day do not stumble, because
they see the light of this world.
10But those who walk at night
stumble, because the light is not
in them." 11After saying this, he
told them, "Our friend Lazarus
has fallen asleep, but I am going
there to awaken him." 12The
disciples said to him, "Lord, if
he has fallen asleep, he will be
all right." 13Jesus, however, had
been speaking about his death,
but they thought that he was
referring merely to sleep. 14Then
Jesus told them plainly, "Lazarus
is dead. 15For your sake I am glad
I was not there, so that you may
believe. But let us go to him."
16Thomas, who was called the
Twin, said to his fellow disciples,
"Let us also go, that we may die
with him."

17When Jesus arrived, he found
that Lazarus had already been
in the tomb four days. 18Now
Bethany was near Jerusalem,
some two miles away, 19and many
of the Jews had come to Martha
and Mary to console them about
their brother. 20When Martha
heard that Jesus was coming, she
went and met him, while Mary
stayed at home. 21Martha said
to Jesus, "Lord, if you had been
here, my brother would not have
died. 22But even now I know that
God will give you whatever you
ask of him." 23Jesus said to her,
"Your brother will rise again."
24Martha said to him, "I know
that he will rise again in the
resurrection on the last day."
25Jesus said to her, "I am the
resurrection and the life. Those
who believe in me, even though
they die, will live, 26and everyone
who lives and believes in me will
never die. Do you believe this?"
27She said to him, "Yes, Lord, I
believe that you are the Messiah,
the Son of God, the one coming
into the world."

28When she had said this, she
went back and called her sister
Mary, and told her privately,
"The Teacher is here and is
calling for you." 29And when
she heard it, she got up quickly
and went to him. 30Now Jesus
had not yet come to the village,
but was still at the place where
Martha had met him. 31The
Jews who were with her in the
house, consoling her, saw Mary
get up quickly and go out.
They followed her because they
thought that she was going to
the tomb to weep there. 32When
Mary came where Jesus was and
saw him, she knelt at his feet and
said to him, "Lord, if you had
been here, my brother would not
have died." 33When Jesus saw
her weeping, and the Jews who
came with her also weeping, he
was greatly disturbed in spirit
and deeply moved. 34He said,
"Where have you laid him?"
They said to him, "Lord, come
and see." 35Jesus began to weep.
36So the Jews said, "See how he
loved him!" 37But some of them

said, "Could not he who opened
the eyes of the blind man have
kept this man from dying?"

38Then Jesus, again greatly
disturbed, came to the tomb.
It was a cave, and a stone was
lying against it. 39Jesus said,
"Take away the stone." Martha,
the sister of the dead man, said
to him, "Lord, already there is
a stench because he has been
dead four days." 40Jesus said
to her, "Did I not tell you that
if you believed, you would see
the glory of God?" 41So they
took away the stone. And Jesus
looked upward and said, "Father,
I thank you for having heard me.
42I knew that you always hear
me, but I have said this for the
sake of the crowd standing here,
so that they may believe that you
sent me." 43When he had said
this, he cried with a loud voice,
"Lazarus, come out!" 44The dead
man came out, his hands and
feet bound with strips of cloth,
and his face wrapped in a cloth.
Jesus said to them, "Unbind him,
and let him go."

Reflection

Some people read the miracles of Jesus literally and historically—if the Bible says that Jesus raised Lazarus from the dead, then it actually happened. Contrast that with the Jesus Seminar, a group of scholars who debate and dissect the authenticity of any passage in the gospels containing a miracle. However we understand miracles though, few are bigger or more challenging for readers than the one in this passage.

The Gospel of John is written so that its hearers may believe in Jesus. Jesus also tells his disciples that his action in this moment is "so that you may believe." But when Lazarus steps forth from the tomb, those looking on can scarcely believe what they're seeing.

The raising of Lazarus represents challenges for us, as well. Will we embrace this Jesus and the awe-inspiring power he represents? Or will we too let this divine power disturb us so mightily that we try to minimize, ignore, or subvert it?

Ultimately, whether we think that Jesus literally raised a beloved friend from the dead or understand the story as symbolic of Jesus' central role in God's transformation of the cosmos, it seems that we too are called to believe something powerful and transformative. Perhaps we might say it in this way: The raising of Lazarus is a story that tells us God holds ultimate power over life and death. In the hands of a loving God, the end of things is never the end.

Dr. Greg Garrett
Professor of English at Baylor University
Writer in Residence at the Seminary of the Southwest
Austin, Texas

Questions

When in your own life have you seen life triumph over death? When have you seen such moments in your faith community? How can we tell those stories of how God brings life out of death?

Prayer

Holy One of Blessing, we long to live in the knowledge and love of you. Help us to know and to believe in the one who triumphed over death that we might know real life, your Son, our Savior, Jesus Christ. *Amen.*

Day 27

John 11:45-57

[45]Many of the Jews therefore,
who had come with Mary and
had seen what Jesus did, believed
in him. [46]But some of them went
to the Pharisees and told them
what he had done. [47]So the chief
priests and the Pharisees called
a meeting of the council, and
said, "What are we to do? This
man is performing many signs.
[48]If we let him go on like this,
everyone will believe in him,
and the Romans will come and
destroy both our holy place and
our nation." [49]But one of them,
Caiaphas, who was high priest
that year, said to them, "You
know nothing at all! [50]You do
not understand that it is better
for you to have one man die
for the people than to have the
whole nation destroyed." [51]He
did not say this on his own, but
being high priest that year he
prophesied that Jesus was about
to die for the nation, [52]and not
for the nation only, but to gather
into one the dispersed children of
God. [53]So from that day on they
planned to put him to death.

[54]Jesus therefore no longer
walked about openly among
the Jews, but went from there
to a town called Ephraim in
the region near the wilderness;
and he remained there with the
disciples.

[55]Now the Passover of the Jews
was near, and many went up
from the country to Jerusalem
before the Passover to purify
themselves. [56]They were looking
for Jesus and were asking one
another as they stood in the
temple, "What do you think?
Surely he will not come to the
festival, will he?" [57]Now the chief
priests and the Pharisees had
given orders that anyone who
knew where Jesus was should let
them know, so that they might
arrest him.

Reflection

The plot thickens. Tension is mounting. The Pharisees and chief priests plot to arrest Jesus and have him killed. Caiaphas famously says, "It is better for you to have one man die for the people than to have the whole nation destroyed." How little he knows.

Try for a moment to put aside what you know is coming, and what you know is the real significance of these words. Imagine yourself in Roman-occupied Jerusalem, where a very uneasy peace is brutally enforced and fear permeates daily life.

The high priests and Pharisees are threatened by Jesus. Who is this man? And what do his claims mean for their own authority? Even more: What do his claims mean for an oppressed people desperately hoping for a Messiah? Will he, can he, bring about God's promised kingdom? And does this mean deliverance from the Romans, a restored Israel, and a king like David?

This kind of revolution, with or without a Messiah, would mean blood in the streets—a lot of it. Thirty years later, there really was a rebellion against Rome, and it ended very, very badly, with thousands dead, the temple destroyed, and blood in the streets.

So think about this: Was Caiaphas right? Not in any theological sense, but in the reality of his situation? What would you do? Would it be better to preserve the peace, however uneasy, than for many to die?

We would never act like Caiaphas, right? Hmmm. Think about it. How have you reacted when challenged or threatened?

The Very Rev. Lucinda Laird
Dean of the American Cathedral
Paris, France

Questions

It has been said that the opposite of faith is not doubt but fear. What do you think? Do you agree?

Prayer

Gracious God, open our hearts and minds to know in the depths of our being that you are always with us and that you hold us in your never-ending love. In times of fear and threat especially, help us to hear your voice and to be channels of your peace. *Amen.*

John 12:1-11

12 Six days before the Passover Jesus came to Bethany, the home of Lazarus, whom he had raised from the dead. 2There they gave a dinner for him. Martha served, and Lazarus was one of those at the table with him. 3Mary took a pound of costly perfume made of pure nard, anointed Jesus' feet, and wiped them with her hair. The house was filled with the fragrance of the perfume. 4But Judas Iscariot, one of his disciples (the one who was about to betray him), said, 5"Why was this perfume not sold for three hundred denarii and the money given to the poor?" 6(He said this not because he cared about the poor, but because he was a thief; he kept the common purse and used to steal what was put into it.) 7Jesus said, "Leave her alone. She bought it so that she might keep it for the day of my burial. 8You always have the poor with you, but you do not always have me." 9When the great crowd of the Jews learned that he was there, they came not only because of Jesus but also to see Lazarus, whom he had raised from the dead. 10So the chief priests planned to put Lazarus to death as well, 11since it was on account of him that many of the Jews were deserting and were believing in Jesus.

Reflection

In this time of fear and mounting tension, Jesus does what most of us would do: He goes to be with his friends. Mary, Martha, and Lazarus seem to be his second family. We are told that he loved Martha, her sister, and Lazarus, and it is to Martha that he proclaims, "I am the resurrection and the life." Jesus goes to Bethany to be with them, and, as you or I might, they give a dinner for him.

Martha serves—of course she does. If we remember Luke's description of her, we know that she would. Perhaps she has been cooking and cleaning all day, to do everything she can, to offer her very best to Jesus. This is her gift of love, and, while the text does not say so, we can be sure Jesus knows this and values it.

Mary's gift is much more out of the ordinary—it is, in fact, startling. Not only is the perfume of pure nard that she pours over his feet extremely expensive but also the way she does it is way out of line. Wiping his feet with her hair is incredibly intimate—and frankly, rather scandalous.

Mary doesn't care. The intimacy, the drama, the wild extravagance—she must express her love, her care, her concern. She does all that she can, and Jesus sees and understands.

God's love for us is extravagant, abundant, overflowing. Sometimes it is even almost embarrassing. Can our response be similar?

The Very Rev. Lucinda Laird
Dean of the American Cathedral
Paris, France

Question

Do you remember a time when you felt so full of love for someone else that you could act like Mary did with Jesus? If your response is, "Not since I was a teenager," think about asking God to open you up to know how you are loved and can love.

Prayer

Gracious God, you have loved us into being and will love us into eternity. Fill our hearts so that we may know this truly and respond in kind. May our love for you overflow into love for all your children and all creation. *Amen.*

Day 29

John 12:12-26

12 The next day the great crowd that had come to the festival heard that Jesus was coming to Jerusalem. 13 So they took branches of palm trees and went out to meet him, shouting, "Hosanna! Blessed is the one who comes in the name of the Lord— the King of Israel!" 14 Jesus found a young donkey and sat on it; as it is written: 15 "Do not be afraid, daughter of Zion. Look, your king is coming, sitting on a donkey's colt!"

16 His disciples did not understand these things at first; but when Jesus was glorified, then they remembered that these things had been written of him and had been done to him. 17 So the crowd that had been with him when he called Lazarus out of the tomb and raised him from the dead continued to testify. 18 It was also because they heard that he had performed this sign that the crowd went to meet him. 19 The Pharisees then said to one another, "You see, you can do nothing. Look, the world has gone after him!"

20 Now among those who went up to worship at the festival were some Greeks. 21 They came to Philip, who was from Bethsaida in Galilee, and said to him, "Sir, we wish to see Jesus." 22 Philip went and told Andrew; then Andrew and Philip went and told Jesus. 23 Jesus answered them, "The hour has come for the Son of Man to be glorified. 24 Very truly, I tell you, unless a grain of wheat falls into the earth and dies, it remains just a single grain; but if it dies, it bears much fruit. 25 Those who love their life lose it, and those who hate their life in this world will keep it for eternal life. 26 Whoever serves me must follow me, and where I am, there will my servant be also. Whoever serves me, the Father will honor.

Reflection

Jesus enters Jerusalem and creates quite a stir. His followers are gathered about him, shouting words of praise and longing for the culmination of something significant. There he is, among branches of palm, riding a donkey. We call this the triumphal entry of Jesus into the holy city of Jerusalem.

The ancients knew something about triumphs. Military celebrations, following victories of note on the field of battle, were common. A triumph honored soldiers but especially the general who led the troops. History tells of many such celebrations. On occasion, a tangible monument of the victory was erected; Rome is home to numerous arches and columns that serve as symbols of victory. Humans like solid reminders of our victories.

When we view Jesus' prophetic triumph, we can't help but consider it in contrast to the examples of Roman triumph. We see no chariots, war horses, or weapons. We see a first-century Jew with his friends and followers, waving palms. This is a different sort of celebration.

Maybe this is the point: Jesus' entry stands in opposition to grandeur and the usual signs of might. The concrete reminder of this triumph is solid and lasting. It is no column or arch. It is the cross. It is not so much about the power of victory as it is the power of sacrificial love.

The Rev. Christopher L. Epperson
Rector of Bruton Parish Church
Williamsburg, Virginia

Question

In a world that values strength, how can we witness to the power of sacrifice?

Prayer

Almighty God, we know your power chiefly in your creative and redemptive love. As we seek to be faithful to your call, help us to remember that your Son embodied humility and self-giving love. Show us the way to embody his witness and to seek your way of power and glory. *Amen.*

DAY 30

John 12:27-50

27“Now my soul is troubled. And what should I say—‘Father, save me from this hour’? No, it is for this reason that I have come to this hour. 28Father, glorify your name.” Then a voice came from heaven, “I have glorified it, and I will glorify it again.” 29The crowd standing there heard it and said that it was thunder. Others said, “An angel has spoken to him.” 30Jesus answered, “This voice has come for your sake, not for mine. 31Now is the judgment of this world; now the ruler of this world will be driven out. 32And I, when I am lifted up from the earth, will draw all people to myself.” 33He said this to indicate the kind of death he was to die. 34The crowd answered him, “We have heard from the law that the Messiah remains forever. How can you say that the Son of Man must be lifted up? Who is this Son of Man?” 35Jesus said to them, “The light is with you for a little longer. Walk while you have the light, so that the darkness may not overtake you. If you walk in the darkness, you do not know where you are going. 36While you have the light, believe in the light, so that you may become children of light.”

After Jesus had said this, he departed and hid from them. 37Although he had performed so many signs in their presence, they did not believe in him. 38This was to fulfill the word spoken by the prophet Isaiah: “Lord, who has believed our message, and to whom has the arm of the Lord been revealed?” 39And so they could not believe, because Isaiah also said, 40“He has blinded their eyes and hardened their heart, so that they might not look with their eyes, and understand with their heart and turn—and I would heal them." [41]Isaiah said this because he saw his glory and spoke about him.

[42]Nevertheless many, even of the authorities, believed in him. But because of the Pharisees they did not confess it, for fear that they would be put out of the synagogue; [43]for they loved human glory more than the glory that comes from God.

[44]Then Jesus cried aloud: "Whoever believes in me believes not in me but in him who sent me. [45]And whoever sees me sees him who sent me. [46]I have come as light into the world, so that everyone who believes in me should not remain in the darkness. [47]I do not judge anyone who hears my words and does not keep them, for I came not to judge the world, but to save the world. [48]The one who rejects me and does not receive my word has a judge; on the last day the word that I have spoken will serve as judge, [49]for I have not spoken on my own, but the Father who sent me has himself given me a commandment about what to say and what to speak. [50]And I know that his commandment is eternal life. What I speak, therefore, I speak just as the Father has told me."

Reflection

Good communicators, teachers, and leaders possess thoughtful ways of connecting a moment in time to the larger arc of the story, lesson, or mission. Hearers and followers need to be reminded of the larger picture to understand; engagement with the meta narrative keeps people attentive, focused, and engaged.

Jesus' disciples and the gathered crowds have seen and heard so much from Jesus. Signs and teachings fill the Gospel according to John. Jesus does and says so much. The Fourth Gospel recognizes how easy it might be for the reader to become lost along the way, so the author of the Fourth Gospel offers us a moment to regain our bearings.

We witness Jesus at a pivotal moment in his ministry. Jesus knows that his followers need to be grounded for the journey ahead of them. Jesus reminds them of the journey they have been sharing, what it means, and where they are heading. The followers (and the readers) need to remember what this moment is all about—the bigger picture.

Darkness is real, but it always gives way to light. All are invited into the light, but some will choose to remain blind. It is the Way. It is our way. Jesus comes that all might see. We are offered the opportunity to see nothing less than God in Christ.

This Jesus is no mere wisdom teacher, no simple hypnotist healer. This Jesus is God.

The Rev. Christopher L. Epperson
Rector of Bruton Parish Church
Williamsburg, Virginia

Questions

In the changes and chances of this life, do we remember that we participate in a larger narrative of God's redemption of creation? What difference would it make if we viewed all of life through that lens?

Prayer

Lord God, you came that we might know and serve you as you break down the chasm that separates us from you. Grant us the ability to see and know your redeeming and unifying work. Help us respond to your efforts, when we see and know. Bind us together in the body of your son, Jesus Christ, Our Lord. *Amen.*

DAY 31

John 13:1-20

13 Now before the festival of the Passover, Jesus knew that his hour had come to depart from this world and go to the Father. Having loved his own who were in the world, he loved them to the end. 2The devil had already put it into the heart of Judas son of Simon Iscariot to betray him. And during supper 3Jesus, knowing that the Father had given all things into his hands, and that he had come from God and was going to God, 4got up from the table, took off his outer robe, and tied a towel around himself. 5Then he poured water into a basin and began to wash the disciples' feet and to wipe them with the towel that was tied around him. 6He came to Simon Peter, who said to him, "Lord, are you going to wash my feet?" 7Jesus answered, "You do not know now what I am doing, but later you will understand." 8Peter said to him, "You will never wash my feet." Jesus answered, "Unless I wash you, you have no share with me." 9Simon Peter said to him, "Lord, not my feet only but also my hands and my head!" 10Jesus said to him, "One who has bathed does not need to wash, except for the feet, but is entirely clean. And you are clean, though not all of you." 11For he knew who was to betray him; for this reason he said, "Not all of you are clean."

12After he had washed their feet, had put on his robe, and had returned to the table, he said to them, "Do you know what I have done to you? 13You call me Teacher and Lord—and you are right, for that is what I am. 14So if I, your Lord and Teacher, have washed your feet, you also ought to wash one another's feet. 15For I have set you an example, that you also should do as I have

done to you. 16 Very truly, I tell
you, servants are not greater than
their master, nor are messengers
greater than the one who sent
them. 17 If you know these things,
you are blessed if you do them.

18 I am not speaking of all of you;
I know whom I have chosen. But
it is to fulfill the scripture, 'The
one who ate my bread has lifted
his heel against me.' 19 I tell you
this now, before it occurs, so
that when it does occur, you may
believe that I am he. 20 Very truly,
I tell you, whoever receives one
whom I send receives me; and
whoever receives me receives him
who sent me."

Reflection

After a day of walking, a tired pilgrim sits by a clear stream in the fading light of day. He tenderly places his aching and dusty feet into the rushing current. He exhales and allows the living water to cleanse and heal his body.

The apostles are nearing the end of their journey with Jesus. With each step, they have witnessed love, healing, inclusion, and miracles—simultaneously struggling with their own egos and questions. They sit, and in the fading light of day, Jesus reaches out to cleanse their lives in the healing waters of his touch. Peter questions and protests, and it is easy to understand why. To become vulnerable is the dilemma we face in a world that values topical solutions. It is simpler to hide our blistered and gnarled lives than to place them in the healing hands of the Lord. We wonder and protest because to do otherwise requires vulnerability and the loss of independence. This passage reminds us that our way in this world is only made by walking with the Lord.

The journey can be tiresome and dusty, yet with each step is a knowing that Christ will always reach out. By placing our feet and our lives into his hands, we discover that living waters heal. Imagine the healing Jesus brings when he takes your life into his hands. He pours the water and then soothes all the pain. In his healing hands, you are prepared for your journey.

The Rt. Rev. Daniel G. P. Gutierrez
Bishop of the Episcopal Diocese of Pennsylvania
Philadelphia, Pennsylvania

Question

When do you sit and place yourself in the hands of Christ? Reflect on instances when you were healed spiritually and physically.

Prayer

O Most Holy One, give us the presence to sit and place our lives into your hands. Help us to place all that we have—the pain, the joy, the journey—into your gentle hands. Let us sit and feel the healing waters wash away all the pain. *Amen.*

DAY 32

John 13:21-38

21After saying this Jesus was troubled in spirit, and declared, "Very truly, I tell you, one of you will betray me." 22The disciples looked at one another, uncertain of whom he was speaking. 23One of his disciples—the one whom Jesus loved—was reclining next to him; 24Simon Peter therefore motioned to him to ask Jesus of whom he was speaking. 25So while reclining next to Jesus, he asked him, "Lord, who is it?" 26Jesus answered, "It is the one to whom I give this piece of bread when I have dipped it in the dish." So when he had dipped the piece of bread, he gave it to Judas son of Simon Iscariot. 27After he received the piece of bread, Satan entered into him. Jesus said to him, "Do quickly what you are going to do." 28Now no one at the table knew why he said this to him. 29Some thought that, because Judas had the common purse, Jesus was telling him, "Buy what we need for the festival"; or, that he should give something to the poor. 30So, after receiving the piece of bread, he immediately went out. And it was night.

31When he had gone out, Jesus said, "Now the Son of Man has been glorified, and God has been glorified in him. 32If God has been glorified in him, God will also glorify him in himself and will glorify him at once. 33Little children, I am with you only a little longer. You will look for me; and as I said to the Jews so now I say to you, 'Where I am going, you cannot come.' 34I give you a new commandment, that you love one another. Just as I have loved you, you also should love one another. 35By this everyone will know that you are my disciples, if you have love for one another."

[36]Simon Peter said to him, "Lord,
where are you going?" Jesus
answered, "Where I am going,
you cannot follow me now;
but you will follow afterward."
[37]Peter said to him, "Lord, why
can I not follow you now? I will
lay down my life for you." [38]Jesus
answered, "Will you lay down
your life for me? Very truly, I tell
you, before the cock crows, you
will have denied me three times.

Reflection

Trust affects relationships, bringing people closer or tearing them apart. With elements of power and vulnerability, faith and giving up control, the issue of trust hangs heavily over the table on this sacred night in the upper room. Sitting with his friends, Jesus kneels and washes the feet of the Apostles; he has journeyed with them and loved them. Jesus knows one will betray him, and all but one will abandon him. Yet Jesus continues to trust: those at the table, his mission, and his Father.

Jesus' example speaks to the importance of trust in our lives today. We are called into relationship with a loving God who continually reinforces our confidence in him. Jesus turns to the Father and knows the truth. He is never suspicious, guarded, or seeking assurance. Jesus lives a life open to the Father. Jesus teaches us to believe that we will be held up even if we let go—that we should live a life that is giving, holy, and transformative.

Jesus exemplifies trust, because Jesus is always in close relationship with the Father. He spends regular time in prayer. Relationship with the Father relieves Jesus of suspicion, anxiety, and fear. Prayer speaks to the loving heart of the Father, and Jesus trusts his Father's love. The darkness of distrust and fear gives way to the light of faith and love. Like Jesus, a faithful people see life from the perspective of trust and love, not fear or control.

The Rt. Rev. Daniel G. P. Gutierrez
Bishop of the Episcopal Diocese of Pennsylvania
Philadelphia, Pennsylvania

Question

In a world filled with uncertainty, where can you find hope? Examine the instances in your life when you opened your life to God and trusted.

Prayer

O Most Holy One, amidst the changing and uncertain times, allow us to trust in your never-ending love. When we look to you, our fear turns to faith and our control turns to love. Only you are never changing. *Amen.*

DAY 33

John 14:1-14

14 "Do not let your hearts be troubled. Believe in God, believe also in me. 2In my Father's house there are many dwelling places. If it were not so, would I have told you that I go to prepare a place for you? 3And if I go and prepare a place for you, I will come again and will take you to myself, so that where I am, there you may be also. 4And you know the way to the place where I am going." 5Thomas said to him, "Lord, we do not know where you are going. How can we know the way?" 6Jesus said to him, "I am the way, and the truth, and the life. No one comes to the Father except through me. 7If you know me, you will know my Father also. From now on you do know him and have seen him."

8Philip said to him, "Lord, show us the Father, and we will be satisfied." 9Jesus said to him, "Have I been with you all this time, Philip, and you still do not know me? Whoever has seen me has seen the Father. How can you say, 'Show us the Father'? 10Do you not believe that I am in the Father and the Father is in me? The words that I say to you I do not speak on my own; but the Father who dwells in me does his works. 11Believe me that I am in the Father and the Father is in me; but if you do not, then believe me because of the works themselves. 12"Very truly, I tell you, the one who believes in me will also do the works that I do and, in fact, will do greater works than these, because I am going to the Father. 13I will do whatever you ask in my name, so that the Father may be glorified in the Son. 14If in my name you ask me for anything, I will do it."

Reflection

Jesus has just announced he is leaving. The disciples feel frightened and lonely, abandoned. Departures are never easy.

Recently I had an experience that brought this moment in the Bible home to me. When I arrived at border control in the United States, after traveling from Madrid, a policeman took my passport and asked me some questions about the purpose of my visit and where I would be staying. Then he told me to follow him. I went to a very dark room full of people from other countries. Everyone looked scared and nervous. He said, "You must wait here."

I waited one hour. After an hour, I asked him how much longer. Three hours passed. I felt alone. Disoriented. Fearful, I wondered, "What will happen to me?"

In that moment, I thought of this passage and the moment when Jesus says to his disciples: "Do not let your hearts be troubled. Believe in God, believe also in me." Peace came over me. I was reminded that I was following God's will to the best of my ability.

Sometimes life feels complicated and difficult, especially when traveling from one country to another. Just after I experienced this moment of surrender in the promise of Jesus, the policeman returned my passport and explained that a new law had caused the temporary detainment. I was given permission both to enter the United States and to return eventually to Spain. I walked out of the airport tired but with a certain confidence. There is never a reason for my heart to be troubled; Jesus reminds me over and over again.

The Rt. Rev. Carlos López-Lozano
Bishop of the Reformed Episcopal Church of Spain
Madrid, Spain

Questions

Have you felt afraid, uncertain, or disoriented in your life? How difficult have you found it to trust in these moments?

Prayer

Lord, help me when I am traveling and when my heart is full of fears. Give me confidence, which comes from my faith in you that you will guide me and lead me and protect me all the days of my life. *Amen.*

DAY 34

John 14:15-31

15"If you love me, you will keep
my commandments. 16And I will
ask the Father, and he will give
you another Advocate, to be with
you forever. 17This is the Spirit of
truth, whom the world cannot
receive, because it neither sees
him nor knows him. You know
him, because he abides with you,
and he will be in you.

18"I will not leave you orphaned;
I am coming to you. 19In a little
while the world will no longer
see me, but you will see me;
because I live, you also will live.
20On that day you will know that
I am in my Father, and you in
me, and I in you. 21They who
have my commandments and
keep them are those who love
me; and those who love me will
be loved by my Father, and I will
love them and reveal myself to
them." 22Judas (not Iscariot) said
to him, "Lord, how is it that you
will reveal yourself to us, and not
to the world?" 23Jesus answered
him, "Those who love me will
keep my word, and my Father
will love them, and we will come
to them and make our home
with them. 24Whoever does not
love me does not keep my words;
and the word that you hear is not
mine, but is from the Father who
sent me.

25"I have said these things to you
while I am still with you. 26But
the Advocate, the Holy Spirit,
whom the Father will send in my
name, will teach you everything,
and remind you of all that I have
said to you. 27Peace I leave with
you; my peace I give to you. I
do not give to you as the world
gives. Do not let your hearts be
troubled, and do not let them
be afraid. 28"You heard me say
to you, 'I am going away, and I
am coming to you.' If you loved
me, you would rejoice that I am
going to the Father, because the

Father is greater than I. [29]And
now I have told you this before
it occurs, so that when it does
occur, you may believe. [30]I will
no longer talk much with you, for
the ruler of this world is coming.
He has no power over me; [31]but I
do as the Father has commanded
me, so that the world may know
that I love the Father. Rise, let us
be on our way."

Reflection

A few months ago, we tried to restore the building next to the cathedral where we have our food distribution program and our parish council meetings. It was in great need of repair. I filed numerous requests with town hall. Many went unanswered. I left several messages. After more than twenty-five communications to obtain permission to restore the building and still no answers, I felt very disheartened. I was in an anxious state. The building was in bad shape.

Perhaps if you are in a similar situation you might recall as I did these two verses from chapter 14 from the Gospel of John. Verse 16: "And I will ask the Father, and he will give you another Advocate, to be with you forever." And verse 27: "Peace I leave with you; my peace I give you. I do not give to you as the world gives. Do not let your hearts be troubled, and do not let them be afraid." In Greek, the word advocate (or counselor) is *parákletos*, which means the one who is next to you to support and help you. I realized again I was *not* alone. And I am reminded of Jesus' promise of peace because we sing it in Spanish every Sunday: *La paz os dejo, Mi paz os doy*...Peace is always there with me if I am listening and looking for it.

The truth is nothing goes quickly in Spain! After more paperwork and another sixty days, I still had no solution, but I carried on better because these verses helped me. Four months later, restoration began.

The Rt. Rev. Carlos López-Lozano
Bishop of the Reformed Episcopal Church of Spain
Madrid, Spain

Questions

Have you been challenged by a lack of patience in your life? Where do you turn for solace? Do you feel the Holy Spirit as a presence in your life?

Prayer

Thank you, Lord, for giving us your Holy Spirit as our support, to console us and to give us energy to go forward. Thank you, Lord, for this Holy Spirit that comes down upon us and gives us peace. Truly we need it. *Amen.*

DAY 35

John 15:1-17

15 "I am the true vine,
and my Father is the
vinegrower. 2He removes every
branch in me that bears no
fruit. Every branch that bears
fruit he prunes to make it bear
more fruit. 3You have already
been cleansed by the word that
I have spoken to you. 4Abide
in me as I abide in you. Just as
the branch cannot bear fruit by
itself unless it abides in the vine,
neither can you unless you abide
in me. 5I am the vine, you are
the branches. Those who abide
in me and I in them bear much
fruit, because apart from me you
can do nothing. 6Whoever does
not abide in me is thrown away
like a branch and withers; such
branches are gathered, thrown
into the fire, and burned. 7If
you abide in me, and my words
abide in you, ask for whatever
you wish, and it will be done for
you. 8My Father is glorified by
this, that you bear much fruit
and become my disciples. 9As the
Father has loved me, so I have
loved you; abide in my love. 10If
you keep my commandments,
you will abide in my love,
just as I have kept my Father's
commandments and abide in his
love. 11I have said these things
to you so that my joy may be in
you, and that your joy may be
complete.

12"This is my commandment,
that you love one another as I
have loved you. 13No one has
greater love than this, to lay
down one's life for one's friends.
14You are my friends if you do
what I command you. 15I do
not call you servants any longer,
because the servant does not
know what the master is doing;
but I have called you friends,
because I have made known to
you everything that I have heard
from my Father. 16You did not
choose me but I chose you. And

ointed you to go and bear fruit that will last, so that the Father will give you whatever you ask him in my name. [17]I am giving you these commands so that you may love one another."

Reflection

One early translation into Syriac of "I am the true vine" is "I am the Vineyard of the Truth." Although this is a misreading of the Greek "vine" (*ámpelos* rather than *ampelón*, which means vineyard), the rendering is nonetheless powerful. Jesus is not only the source of all life but also of all truth. Put another way: Jesus gives the power to live truthfully because he is truth incarnate. To know what is true, we need to look to Jesus; we need to find our life in him.

This emphasis on the truth resonates with other passages in John's Gospel. To pick a few: Jesus is the "Word become flesh" that is "full of grace and truth" (1:14). Jesus says, "I am the way, and the truth, and the life" (14:6) and promises a few verses later that we will be guided by the Spirit of truth. At Jesus' trial, Pilate asks, "What is truth?" (18:38), indicating that he does not see the truth hidden in plain sight in the person of Jesus.

We tend to think of truth as an object of scientific study or philosophical argument. In John, truth is a relationship. To know the truth, we need to know Jesus. His truth is love. His truth is life. His truth is found in friendship with him. Knowing Jesus is not an intellectual achievement but rather a spiritual reality. This is why the vine metaphor is so appropriate, because relationships, like plants, need to be tended so that they may thrive and grow.

The Rev. Dr. William J. Danaher Jr.
Rector of Christ Church Cranbrook
Bloomfield Hills, Michigan

Questions

What is the truth that guides your life? How can you let the truth of Jesus grow deeper inside you?

Prayer

Jesus, our true vine, help us see your truth. May your truth set us free to know and love you, so that, by your grace, the world may know you as we do. May your truth grow in us so that we might see you always. *Amen.*

DAY 36

John 15:18-27

18“If the world hates you, be aware that it hated me before it hated you. 19If you belonged to the world, the world would love you as its own. Because you do not belong to the world, but I have chosen you out of the world—therefore the world hates you. 20Remember the word that I said to you, ‘Servants are not greater than their master.’ If they persecuted me, they will persecute you; if they kept my word, they will keep yours also. 21But they will do all these things to you on account of my name, because they do not know him who sent me. 22If I had not come and spoken to them, they would not have sin; but now they have no excuse for their sin. 23Whoever hates me hates my Father also. 24If I had not done among them the works that no one else did, they would not have sin. But now they have seen and hated both me and my Father. 25It was to fulfill the word that is written in their law, ‘They hated me without a cause.’

26“When the Advocate comes, whom I will send to you from the Father, the Spirit of truth who comes from the Father, he will testify on my behalf. 27You also are to testify because you have been with me from the beginning.”

Reflection

We live in polarizing times. Politicians and preachers like to separate people into opposing groups—us against them, good against evil, right against wrong. From one perspective, Jesus' language about the world's hatred seems like more of the same. If so, this rhetoric is disturbing. Binaries like this usually justify the marginalization of the poor and the weak among us as outsiders less worthy of love and respect.

In other scriptures and in John's Gospel, Jesus' ministry is described as an exercise in God's love for the world. "In Christ," we read, "God was reconciling the world to himself...and entrusting the message of reconciliation to us" (2 Corinthians 5:19). And in the famous passage from John 3:16, "For God so loved the world that he gave his only Son, so that everyone who believes in him may not perish but may have eternal life."

Jesus' words about the world must be read, then, in light of these other expressions of loyalty to the world. Saint Augustine believed that the precise meaning of the world depended on whether or not one was a follower of Jesus: The "world condemned persecutes; the world reconciled suffers persecution."

The real question, then, is whether or not our lives conform to Christ's love and life. Jesus made enemies in this world because of his justice—his willingness to stand with the poor and the outcast. Jesus loved the world, even in the face of resistance and death. May his grace transform us and bridge the boundaries between us.

The Rev. Dr. William J. Danaher Jr.
Rector of Christ Church Cranbrook
Bloomfield Hills, Michigan

Questions

How does your relationship with Christ affect your actions in the world—in your immediate context, in your community, in your church? How does the love of Christ challenge the lines we (and others) are prone to draw between insiders and outsiders?

Prayer

Merciful God, we thank you for Jesus, your beloved Son. May we always be challenged by his love, through which he overcomes hate, sin, and death. May his love be our love, his spirit our spirit. Help us to go where his love leads, come what may. *Amen.*

Day 37

John 16:1-15

16 “I have said these things to you to keep you from stumbling. [2]They will put you out of the synagogues. Indeed, an hour is coming when those who kill you will think that by doing so they are offering worship to God. [3]And they will do this because they have not known the Father or me. [4]But I have said these things to you so that when their hour comes you may remember that I told you about them.

“I did not say these things to you from the beginning, because I was with you. [5]But now I am going to him who sent me; yet none of you asks me, ‘Where are you going?’ [6]But because I have said these things to you, sorrow has filled your hearts. [7]Nevertheless I tell you the truth: it is to your advantage that I go away, for if I do not go away, the Advocate will not come to you; but if I go, I will send him to you. [8]And when he comes, he will prove the world wrong about sin and righteousness and judgment: [9]about sin, because they do not believe in me; [10]about righteousness, because I am going to the Father and you will see me no longer; [11]about judgment, because the ruler of this world has been condemned.

[12]“I still have many things to say to you, but you cannot bear them now. [13]When the Spirit of truth comes, he will guide you into all the truth; for he will not speak on his own, but will speak whatever he hears, and he will declare to you the things that are to come. [14]He will glorify me, because he will take what is mine and declare it to you. [15]All that the Father has is mine. For this reason I said that he will take what is mine and declare it to you.”

Reflection

This farewell discourse in John's Gospel can seem dense and cryptic. Its meanings continue to challenge commentators and theologians. Yet these words are full of encouragement to feed souls.

Throughout his last meal with his disciples, Jesus talks them through their discomfort. Jesus has been telling his disciples that he is to go away, that he is to enter into his glory. That glory will come when Jesus is lifted up on the cross. There is sadness around the table as Jesus speaks, and as with the disciples, so too with us. The prospect of being on one's own can be unnerving and frightening. Separation can be a source for sorrow.

Change of any kind always comes with a set of unknowns. It is particularly hard when change means the loss of those closest to us. Who will be in the new place to know us, support us, and care for us?

The disciples do not understand all of what Jesus is saying. He assures them that even though he is leaving, he will send them the Advocate—the Holy Spirit—to lead them into all truth. Separation and loss do not end their relationship. Rather, this change sets up a new occasion for knowing themselves and Jesus even more deeply.

Change opens the way to discover new things about the world and oneself.

The Very Rev. Peter Jay DeVeau
Dean of Grace & Holy Trinity Cathedral
Kansas City, Missouri

Questions

When have you made a change that has brought you into a new and unknown place? What did you learn about yourself? How did you experience God in that time?

Prayer

Jesus, you promised the Holy Spirit to your disciples that they might grow in knowledge of your truth. By the power of that same Spirit, be with us in times of transition to guide us into what is true and lasting. *Amen.*

DAY 38

John 16:16-33

16“A little while, and you will no longer see me, and again a little while, and you will see me.” 17Then some of his disciples said to one another, “What does he mean by saying to us, ‘A little while, and you will no longer see me, and again a little while, and you will see me’; and ‘Because I am going to the Father’?” 18They said, “What does he mean by this ‘a little while’? We do not know what he is talking about.” 19Jesus knew that they wanted to ask him, so he said to them, “Are you discussing among yourselves what I meant when I said, ‘A little while, and you will no longer see me, and again a little while, and you will see me’? 20Very truly, I tell you, you will weep and mourn, but the world will rejoice; you will have pain, but your pain will turn into joy. 21When a woman is in labor, she has pain, because her hour has come. But when her child is born, she no longer remembers the anguish because of the joy of having brought a human being into the world. 22So you have pain now; but I will see you again, and your hearts will rejoice, and no one will take your joy from you. 23On that day you will ask nothing of me. Very truly, I tell you, if you ask anything of the Father in my name, he will give it to you. 24Until now you have not asked for anything in my name. Ask and you will receive, so that your joy may be complete.

25“I have said these things to you in figures of speech. The hour is coming when I will no longer speak to you in figures, but will tell you plainly of the Father. 26On that day you will ask in my name. I do not say to you that I will ask the Father on your behalf; 27for the Father himself loves you, because you have

loved me and have believed that
I came from God. 28I came from
the Father and have come into
the world; again, I am leaving
the world and am going to the
Father."

29His disciples said, "Yes, now
you are speaking plainly, not in
any figure of speech! 30Now we
know that you know all things,
and do not need to have anyone
question you; by this we believe
that you came from God." 31Jesus
answered them, "Do you now
believe? 32The hour is coming,
indeed it has come, when you
will be scattered, each one to
his home, and you will leave
me alone. Yet I am not alone
because the Father is with me. 33I
have said this to you, so that in
me you may have peace. In the
world you face persecution. But
take courage; I have conquered
the world!"

Reflection

Moments after the doctor came to tell us my mother had died, I followed my father to her bedside in the intensive care unit. Her death from spinal meningitis was unexpected and swift. We were numb with grief. In that room bathed in afternoon light, my father looked at his wife's lifeless body and spoke tenderly to her. Thanking her for the time they shared, he stooped to kiss her and said, "I'm not sure what you are seeing or feeling now, but I know we will see each other again."

Jesus speaks his own words of farewell and encouragement to his disciples. He converses with them. He alludes to his cross and to the suffering his disciples are surely to endure. In time, their mourning and weeping will turn to joy. They will see Jesus again.

How do the disciples see Jesus? We may fast forward to that evening on the first day of the week when Jesus appears to his disciples cowering behind locked doors (John 20) or again when he fixes breakfast for them on the beach (John 21). But these scenes are only a beginning. Jesus goes to the Father that he might fulfill all things.

Disciples down through the ages seek and serve Jesus in the people they encounter. He is with us in our pain and all our transitions. He brings joy to our living by his presence.

The Very Rev. Peter Jay DeVeau
Dean of Grace & Holy Trinity Cathedral
Kansas City, Missouri

Questions

How have you seen Christ in times of suffering and loss? Where have you encountered Christ in times of joy?

Prayer

Jesus, speak to us plainly about those things that lead us to you. May our hearts rejoice in you today. *Amen.*

DAY 39

John 17:1-26

17 After Jesus had spoken these words, he looked up to heaven and said, "Father, the hour has come; glorify your Son so that the Son may glorify you, 2since you have given him authority over all people, to give eternal life to all whom you have given him. 3And this is eternal life, that they may know you, the only true God, and Jesus Christ whom you have sent. 4I glorified you on earth by finishing the work that you gave me to do. 5So now, Father, glorify me in your own presence with the glory that I had in your presence before the world existed.

6"I have made your name known to those whom you gave me from the world. They were yours, and you gave them to me, and they have kept your word. 7Now they know that everything you have given me is from you; 8for the words that you gave to me I have given to them, and they have received them and know in truth that I came from you; and they have believed that you sent me. 9I am asking on their behalf; I am not asking on behalf of the world, but on behalf of those whom you gave me, because they are yours. 10All mine are yours, and yours are mine; and I have been glorified in them. 11And now I am no longer in the world, but they are in the world, and I am coming to you. Holy Father, protect them in your name that you have given me, so that they may be one, as we are one. 12While I was with them, I protected them in your name that you have given me. I guarded them, and not one of them was lost except the one destined to be lost, so that the scripture might be fulfilled. 13But now I am coming to you, and I speak these things in the world so that they

may have my joy made complete
in themselves. [14]I have given
them your word, and the world
has hated them because they do
not belong to the world, just as
I do not belong to the world. [15]I
am not asking you to take them
out of the world, but I ask you
to protect them from the evil
one. [16]They do not belong to the
world, just as I do not belong to
the world. [17]Sanctify them in
the truth; your word is truth.
[18]As you have sent me into the
world, so I have sent them into
the world. [19]And for their sakes I
sanctify myself, so that they also
may be sanctified in truth.

[20]"I ask not only on behalf of
these, but also on behalf of those
who will believe in me through
their word, [21]that they may all
be one. As you, Father, are in me
and I am in you, may they also
be in us, so that the world may
believe that you have sent me.
[22]The glory that you have given
me I have given them, so that
they may be one, as we are one,
[23]I in them and you in me, that
they may become completely
one, so that the world may know
that you have sent me and have
loved them even as you have
loved me. [24]Father, I desire that
those also, whom you have given
me, may be with me where I
am, to see my glory, which you
have given me because you loved
me before the foundation of the
world.

[25]"Righteous Father, the world
does not know you, but I know
you; and these know that you
have sent me. [26]I made your
name known to them, and I will
make it known, so that the love
with which you have loved me
may be in them, and I in them."

Reflection

Imagine you are there. Right there. In the midst of Jesus' last moments, you hear this prayer. In his last hours, Jesus prays for his disciples; he prays for us. Incredible. That is Jesus: absolutely incredible.

Even though his disciples do not know what is to come, Jesus does. So for the disciples, he is praying for them, which is amazing in and of itself as an act of love. But for those of us reading this passage today, we see the overarching significance of this moment. Jesus is about to be betrayed, tortured, and killed—and he takes time to pray for his disciples. He prays that they will continue to know the truth and be sanctified by grace, love, and peace.

This is our Savior, who loves us, cares deeply for us, and prays for us. I don't think we ponder this idea enough: Our Lord prays for us. Jesus knows our every need and prays for us as we are praying to him. Prayer is a conversation of sorts. Maybe we need to be quiet more, sit in silence, and listen to the prayer Jesus is praying for us.

The Very Rev. Justin Lindstrom
Dean of Saint Paul's Cathedral
Oklahoma City, Oklahoma

Questions

If you were to listen to Jesus' prayer for you, what might it be? How do you pray for others?

Prayer

Lord Jesus Christ, you hear the prayers of your people, and you know our every need. Help us to hear your prayers for us, that in your words, we may come to know how to follow your will more fully and to love others as you have loved us. In the name of God. *Amen.*

DAY 40

John 18:1-14

18 After Jesus had spoken these words, he went out with his disciples across the Kidron valley to a place where there was a garden, which he and his disciples entered. 2Now Judas, who betrayed him, also knew the place, because Jesus often met there with his disciples. 3So Judas brought a detachment of soldiers together with police from the chief priests and the Pharisees, and they came there with lanterns and torches and weapons. 4Then Jesus, knowing all that was to happen to him, came forward and asked them, "Whom are you looking for?" 5They answered, "Jesus of Nazareth." Jesus replied, "I am he." Judas, who betrayed him, was standing with them. 6When Jesus said to them, "I am he," they stepped back and fell to the ground. 7Again he asked them, "Whom are you looking for?" And they said, "Jesus of Nazareth." 8Jesus answered, "I told you that I am he. So if you are looking for me, let these men go." 9This was to fulfill the word that he had spoken, "I did not lose a single one of those whom you gave me." 10Then Simon Peter, who had a sword, drew it, struck the high priest's slave, and cut off his right ear. The slave's name was Malchus. 11Jesus said to Peter, "Put your sword back into its sheath. Am I not to drink the cup that the Father has given me?"

12So the soldiers, their officer, and the Jewish police arrested Jesus and bound him. 13First they took him to Annas, who was the father-in-law of Caiaphas, the high priest that year. 14Caiaphas was the one who had advised the Jews that it was better to have one person die for the people.

Reflection

This is always a difficult story to hear and read: maybe because it is so violent and jarring or maybe because it is the beginning of a tough road ahead for Jesus. Maybe it is because Jesus knows what is going to happen and still allows it to move forward. Or maybe it is because the betrayal is so hurtful and painful that we hear this story and weep.

We weep for Jesus. We weep for Judas, and we weep for the guards, the high priests, and the Pharisees. We weep for the disciples and others gathered in the garden. We weep because we know what is to come—and it is hard, painful, and hurtful.

Yet, at the same time, we know the rest of the story, as does Jesus. This betrayal must happen for prophecies to be fulfilled, for God's mission of love, grace, and peace to be propagated and for the resurrection to actually take place. Jesus must be betrayed, captured, tried, and crucified on a cross so that on the third day, he can rise from the dead. In all these things, we come to know more fully God's love for us, God's forgiveness for us, and God's hope given to us in the promise of eternal life.

The Very Rev. Justin Lindstrom
Dean of Saint Paul's Cathedral
Oklahoma City, Oklahoma

Questions

As you look out to the world, for what are you weeping this day? What might be happening in your life to make way for something new? What does God need to redeem in your life and in the lives of those around you? How has the betrayal of Jesus and the rest of the passion story changed your life today?

Prayer

Holy and Gracious God, you sent your Son, Jesus Christ, to be betrayed at the hands of those who did not understand and to suffer at the selfishness of the world. Open our hearts and minds to the hurt and pain around us that we may share in all the deep love you have shown us in Christ's sacrifice. Allow us to weep for the world so that we may also have hope for what is to come. In the name of Jesus, Savior and Redeemer of the world, we pray. *Amen.*

DAY 41

John 18:15-27

[15]Simon Peter and another disciple followed Jesus. Since that disciple was known to the high priest, he went with Jesus into the courtyard of the high priest, [16]but Peter was standing outside at the gate. So the other disciple, who was known to the high priest, went out, spoke to the woman who guarded the gate, and brought Peter in. [17]The woman said to Peter, “You are not also one of this man’s disciples, are you?” He said, “I am not.” [18]Now the slaves and the police had made a charcoal fire because it was cold, and they were standing around it and warming themselves. Peter also was standing with them and warming himself.

[19]Then the high priest questioned Jesus about his disciples and about his teaching. [20]Jesus answered, “I have spoken openly to the world; I have always taught in synagogues and in the temple, where all the Jews come together. I have said nothing in secret. [21]Why do you ask me? Ask those who heard what I said to them; they know what I said.” [22]When he had said this, one of the police standing nearby struck Jesus on the face, saying, “Is that how you answer the high priest?” [23]Jesus answered, “If I have spoken wrongly, testify to the wrong. But if I have spoken rightly, why do you strike me?” [24]Then Annas sent him bound to Caiaphas the high priest.

[25]Now Simon Peter was standing and warming himself. They asked him, “You are not also one of his disciples, are you?” He denied it and said, “I am not.” [26]One of the slaves of the high priest, a relative of the man whose ear Peter had cut off, asked, “Did I not see you in the garden with him?” [27]Again Peter denied it, and at that moment the cock crowed.

Reflection

In private and unguarded moments, we tend to slip up and say things we regard as inconsequential. In this passage, we find Peter in one such moment. Peter denies his association with Jesus to the gatekeeper woman, an acquaintance of one of the other disciples. It all happens so quickly, before Peter can pay attention to the question or the one questioning him. A different response from Peter likely would have not had serious consequence. The gatekeeper knows the other disciple, so even if there is any consequence, he can rescue Peter. Yet Peter still denies Jesus.

The nature of sin is such that it often does not seem a big deal at first blush. Once past the moment, in private and after no serious consequence, the sin becomes less of an ordeal. Peter's denial of Jesus the second and third time is probably easier—especially the third time around, when the relative of a man whose ear Peter had injured accuses him of association with Jesus.

All seems well until the moment of awakening when the cost of denial becomes apparent. Denial in human relationship may seem guileless, but it has immense potential to deprive us of the unspeakable joy of affirmation. When the cock in our conscience fails to crow, the pain becomes unbearable and the soul becomes heavy laden. May we choose affirmation over denial in our lives.

The Rev. Canon Isaac Poobalan
Provost and Rector of St. Andrew's Cathedral
Aberdeen, Scotland

Questions

What do we affirm as the core of our faith and our relationship with God? How do we keep God's voice alive and well in our conscience?

Prayer

God of love and compassion who looked upon your servant Peter with abundant love, keep me attentive to your voice that calls tenderly and fill me with the joy of affirming my faith in you, through your Son, Jesus Christ our Lord. *Amen.*

DAY 42

John 18:28-40

28Then they took Jesus from
Caiaphas to Pilate's headquarters. It was early in the
morning. They themselves did
not enter the headquarters, so
as to avoid ritual defilement and
to be able to eat the Passover.
29So Pilate went out to them
and said, "What accusation do
you bring against this man?"
30They answered, "If this man
were not a criminal, we would
not have handed him over to
you." 31Pilate said to them, "Take
him yourselves and judge him
according to your law." The Jews
replied, "We are not permitted
to put anyone to death." 32(This
was to fulfill what Jesus had said
when he indicated the kind of
death he was to die.)

33Then Pilate entered the
headquarters again, summoned
Jesus, and asked him, "Are you
the King of the Jews?" 34Jesus
answered, "Do you ask this on
your own, or did others tell you
about me?" 35Pilate replied, "I am
not a Jew, am I? Your own nation
and the chief priests have handed
you over to me. What have you
done?" 36Jesus answered, "My
kingdom is not from this world.
If my kingdom were from this
world, my followers would be
fighting to keep me from being
handed over to the Jews. But as
it is, my kingdom is not from
here." 37Pilate asked him, "So
you are a king?" Jesus answered,
"You say that I am a king. For
this I was born, and for this I
came into the world, to testify to
the truth. Everyone who belongs
to the truth listens to my voice."
38Pilate asked him, "What is
truth?"

After he had said this, he went
out to the Jews again and told
them, "I find no case against
him. 39But you have a custom
that I release someone for you at
the Passover. Do you want me to
release for you the King of the
Jews?" 40They shouted in reply,
"Not this man, but Barabbas!"
Now Barabbas was a bandit.

Reflection

John the Evangelist captures the heart of the matter with grace and splendor in this complex courtroom drama, when the real power exposes the counterfeit and the ultimate Truth reveals the one searching for truth.

The ritually clean accusers of the Lord remain outside Pilate's courts. So Pilate the ruler becomes the pawn, moving in and out of his own courts. The ritually clean remain outside while the sacramentally clean enter the Court of the Gentile to make all things clean. In this drama of "the ins and the outs," between the ritually clean and the One who will cleanse us all from sin, Pilate discovers the ultimate truth.

John narrates this episode of ultimate judgment on Jesus and treats Pilate with sympathy and compassion. The question put in the mouth of Pilate is framed more as an affirmation of his conviction. In Jesus, Pilate saw truth.

Pilate knew the truth but failed to confess for fear of what it might cost him. We see that truth can be both spoken and unspoken, witnessed in the unblemished life of Christ. So often, we conceal truth in daily life with avoidance, distractions, or escape. Ritual cleanliness was the choice of our Lord's accusers. Our own image of God could be one way we conceal truth today.

The Lord can be no other than the truth. And hence what was said by the psalmist in Psalm 85:11, "Truth shall spring up from the earth," becomes prophetic in the Risen Christ.

The Rev. Canon Isaac Poobalan
Provost and Rector of St. Andrew's Cathedral
Aberdeen, Scotland

Questions

Truth: is it something spoken or lived out? Is it confession in words or lived out in lifestyle? What was in Jesus that even death could not contain?

Prayer

Almighty God, you transform the poverty of our nature by the riches of the grace of Jesus Christ. Quicken in us the life of Jesus, in the way of righteousness to the truth which springs from the earth. *Amen.*

Day 43

John 19:1-16a

19 Then Pilate took Jesus
and had him flogged.
2And the soldiers wove a crown
of thorns and put it on his head,
and they dressed him in a purple
robe. 3They kept coming up
to him, saying, "Hail, King of
the Jews!" and striking him on
the face. 4Pilate went out again
and said to them, "Look, I am
bringing him out to you to let
you know that I find no case
against him." 5So Jesus came
out, wearing the crown of thorns
and the purple robe. Pilate said
to them, "Here is the man!"
6When the chief priests and the
police saw him, they shouted,
"Crucify him! Crucify him!"
Pilate said to them, "Take him
yourselves and crucify him; I
find no case against him." 7The
Jews answered him, "We have a
law, and according to that law
he ought to die because he has
claimed to be the Son of God."
8Now when Pilate heard this, he
was more afraid than ever. 9He
entered his headquarters again
and asked Jesus, "Where are you
from?" But Jesus gave him no
answer. 10Pilate therefore said to
him, "Do you refuse to speak to
me? Do you not know that I have
power to release you, and power
to crucify you?" 11Jesus answered
him, "You would have no power
over me unless it had been given
you from above; therefore the
one who handed me over to you
is guilty of a greater sin." 12From
then on Pilate tried to release
him, but the Jews cried out, "If
you release this man, you are no
friend of the emperor. Everyone
who claims to be a king sets
himself against the emperor."
13When Pilate heard these words,
he brought Jesus outside and sat
on the judge's bench at a place
called The Stone Pavement, or
in Hebrew Gabbatha. 14Now it

was the day of Preparation for
the Passover; and it was about
noon. He said to the Jews, "Here
is your King!" [15]They cried out,
"Away with him! Away with him!
Crucify him!" Pilate asked them,
"Shall I crucify your King?" The
chief priests answered, "We have
no king but the emperor." [16]Then
he handed him over to them to
be crucified.

Reflection

The scene between Jesus and Pilate is a kind of burlesque: *Live! On the Pavement! King Jesus!* The soldiers dress him up like a king, keep asking if he is a king, and then put him in the place of a king. Although most assume that it's Pilate who sits on the judgment seat, it is equally likely that it's Jesus. It would perfect the soldiers' mocking: *Let's put him in the place of a king! Let's put him on the judgment seat!* This is where Jesus begins to judge the people. But it is not the expected judgment. No armies of angels come down, no lightning bolts flash. Instead, Jesus is meek—the Greek word is *praus*.

Praus doesn't mean weakness but rather the strength of God that is under Jesus' control. Although he is designed by the Romans to be the butt of a political joke, Jesus refuses to play his part. Jesus keeps his focus on the final act of the performance, his glorification on a cross.

The shocking judgment from the cross is this: God loves the world and does not condemn it. Instead God comes to his creation as a creature of flesh and blood, is lifted up on the gibbet, and keeps on loving and not condemning. Instead, there is only forgiveness. Even in the face of the very worst thing we can imagine and accomplish, God is at work making everything new.

The Rev. Dr. Paul D. Fromberg
Rector of St. Gregory of Nyssa Episcopal Church
San Francisco, California

Questions

What is the most shocking thing about God's forgiveness? Where in your life do you need to be steadfast in forgiving others?

Prayer

O God, merciful and gracious Savior! Prepare in me a place to welcome your judgment. Release me from my doubt of your love. Free me from the prison built of my indifference and enmity. Come to me as you are revealed in your Son, Jesus Christ. *Amen.*

DAY 44

John 19:16b-30

So they took Jesus; [17]and carrying the cross by himself, he went out to what is called The Place of the Skull, which in Hebrew is called Golgotha. [18]There they crucified him, and with him two others, one on either side, with Jesus between them. [19]Pilate also had an inscription written and put on the cross. It read, "Jesus of Nazareth, the King of the Jews." [20]Many of the Jews read this inscription, because the place where Jesus was crucified was near the city; and it was written in Hebrew, in Latin, and in Greek. [21]Then the chief priests of the Jews said to Pilate, "Do not write, 'The King of the Jews,' but, 'This man said, I am King of the Jews.'" [22]Pilate answered, "What I have written I have written." [23]When the soldiers had crucified Jesus, they took his clothes and divided them into four parts, one for each soldier. They also took his tunic; now the tunic was seamless, woven in one piece from the top. [24]So they said to one another, "Let us not tear it, but cast lots for it to see who will get it." This was to fulfill what the scripture says, "They divided my clothes among themselves, and for my clothing they cast lots." [25]And that is what the soldiers did.

Meanwhile, standing near the cross of Jesus were his mother, and his mother's sister, Mary the wife of Clopas, and Mary Magdalene. [26]When Jesus saw his mother and the disciple whom he loved standing beside her, he said to his mother, "Woman, here is your son." [27]Then he said to the disciple, "Here is your mother." And from that hour the disciple took her into his own home.

[28]After this, when Jesus knew that all was now finished, he said (in order to fulfill the scripture),

"I am thirsty." 29A jar full of sour wine was standing there. So they put a sponge full of the wine on a branch of hyssop and held it to his mouth. 30When Jesus had received the wine, he said, "It is finished." Then he bowed his head and gave up his spirit.

Reflection

Jesus isn't interested in being God's son in order to lord it over us. He doesn't want to be God's son for his own sake. John's Gospel says that Jesus is God's son to the degree that he shows us who God is and what God is like. Jesus goes to his death in order to show us precisely what his Father is like. It is in his broken body that Jesus shows us the perfect image of God.

The body of Jesus is not some sort of costume that God tries on and then takes off. The broken body of Jesus is a part of the eternal nature of God. The broken body that hangs on the cross is who God is—always has been and always will be. This God, Jesus tells us, knows what it means to be betrayed by his friends, knows what it means to be tortured to death in the sight of his mother, knows what it means to die alone.

Jesus is executed for making the claim that God is not distant but is as close to you as your final breath. The truth is, God cannot be distant from us. God is present in our grief and our death. The glory of the cross is Jesus' humble, forgiving, loving presence in the face of the worst thing that human beings can deal out. And when the worst is dealt, Jesus accomplishes his glory, breathing God's Spirit from the cross, recreating us in forgiveness.

The Rev. Dr. Paul D. Fromberg
Rector of St. Gregory of Nyssa Episcopal Church
San Francisco, California

Question

Where do you need God to be present in your life right now?

Prayer

O Constant Love! Come to me in my brokenness and longing heart. Lift my vision to the place where you are always reigning in glory, where I may find my true self. Fill me with your wisdom, that I may speak your peace in the world. Grant this for the sake of him whose throne is a cross, Jesus Christ our Savior. *Amen.*

DAY 45

John 19:31-42

[31]Since it was the day of Preparation, the Jews did not want the bodies left on the cross during the sabbath, especially because that sabbath was a day of great solemnity. So they asked Pilate to have the legs of the crucified men broken and the bodies removed. [32]Then the soldiers came and broke the legs of the first and of the other who had been crucified with him. [33]But when they came to Jesus and saw that he was already dead, they did not break his legs. [34]Instead, one of the soldiers pierced his side with a spear, and at once blood and water came out. [35](He who saw this has testified so that you also may believe. His testimony is true, and he knows that he tells the truth.) [36]These things occurred so that the scripture might be fulfilled, "None of his bones shall be broken." [37]And again another passage of scripture says, "They will look on the one whom they have pierced."

[38]After these things, Joseph of Arimathea, who was a disciple of Jesus, though a secret one because of his fear of the Jews, asked Pilate to let him take away the body of Jesus. Pilate gave him permission; so he came and removed his body. [39]Nicodemus, who had at first come to Jesus by night, also came, bringing a mixture of myrrh and aloes, weighing about a hundred pounds. [40]They took the body of Jesus and wrapped it with the spices in linen cloths, according to the burial custom of the Jews. [41]Now there was a garden in the place where he was crucified, and in the garden there was a new tomb in which no one had ever been laid. [42]And so, because it was the Jewish day of Preparation, and the tomb was nearby, they laid Jesus there.

Reflection

When Jesus talks with the Pharisee Nicodemus earlier in John's Gospel, Nicodemus seems incredulous at the way Jesus speaks about God. He can't get his head around the way Jesus speaks about being born again of water and the spirit. Now blood and water flow from the side of this mysterious man. Jesus is dead, and Nicodemus, at some risk to himself, makes sure that this challenging teacher has the proper customary burial rites.

After all the brutality of scourging, the chaos and horror of the nails of crucifixion, the stench of dying criminals, we are taken to a garden, pungent with the scent of myrrh, aloes, and plants and full of the stone-silence of a newly hewn tomb. John has done this before; a few chapters earlier, after Martha says her brother Lazarus will be stinking after four days in the tomb, John's Gospel gives us the dinner party at which Mary's scented oil fills the house with perfume.

This scene also excites the senses and invites us to immerse ourselves in the moment, to face resolutely the messy reality of torture and death, and then to accompany Jesus, almost as pallbearers ourselves, to a place finally and truly of rest. This ordering of chaos is the movement of the same Spirit who broods over the waters of creation in Genesis and who reveals the presence of God at the heart of all that is.

The Rev. Lucy Winkett
Vicar of St James's Church, Piccadilly
London, England

Questions

Where do you connect with the sense of chaos described in John's Gospel and where do you yearn for rest? Reflect on your relationships, home, work, and decision-making processes. Where do you see this movement of the Spirit is most needed?

Prayer

God who brings order out of chaos, sometimes through surprising people and unforeseen events: Show us how to walk with you more closely from the cross to the garden, from the piercing suffering of life to the peace-making you ask of all of us. In Christ's name. *Amen.*

DAY 46

John 20:1-10

20 Early on the first day of the week, while it was still dark, Mary Magdalene came to the tomb and saw that the stone had been removed from the tomb. 2So she ran and went to Simon Peter and the other disciple, the one whom Jesus loved, and said to them, “They have taken the Lord out of the tomb, and we do not know where they have laid him.” 3Then Peter and the other disciple set out and went toward the tomb. 4The two were running together, but the other disciple outran Peter and reached the tomb first. 5He bent down to look in and saw the linen wrappings lying there, but he did not go in. 6Then Simon Peter came, following him, and went into the tomb. He saw the linen wrappings lying there, 7and the cloth that had been on Jesus’ head, not lying with the linen wrappings but rolled up in a place by itself. 8Then the other disciple, who reached the tomb first, also went in, and he saw and believed; 9for as yet they did not understand the scripture, that he must rise from the dead. 10Then the disciples returned to their homes.

Reflection

That Mary Magdalene finds the will and energy to run from the tomb to tell the others Jesus is missing is a striking and moving detail of the story. Whenever this passage is read, at dawn on Easter Day, outside in the garden of our church in central London, it is amazing to those who are there, bleary-eyed and tired, that Mary Magdalene finds the energy to run. Peter and Simon run too. From the exhaustion and trauma of the crucifixion to the stillness of the next day, when they must have been numb with grief and fear, living, as we learn later, in a locked room because they're afraid: from this stuckness, they are suddenly running. Can it really be true?

Just like the father in Jesus' story of the prodigal son, the first intimation that the One who was dead is alive causes them to run. It is as if they have glimpsed a flash of hope on the horizon, when they thought all had been lost. And they do this in a spirit of inquiry: They do not yet understand the scripture, we are told, and so they are energetically exploring the possibilities after their terrifying ordeal and its catastrophic conclusion. This is one of the effects that new life can have: We fall in love and become unable to sleep. In the midst of new love, we can climb a mountain and sing from the rooftops. We have new and unexpected energy that pulses through us, lifts our heads, and gives us hope.

The Rev. Lucy Winkett
Vicar of St James's Church, Piccadilly
London, England

Question

At the end of this passage, we see the disciples return to their homes. Where or with whom is your home? It may or may not be where you are living now.

Prayer

God of time and eternity, risen from the dead in Christ, help us not to keep looking for you in the empty tombs of our lives but to recognize the new energy you give us to return to our homes alive and free. *Amen.*

DAY 47

John 20:11-23

11But Mary stood weeping outside
the tomb. As she wept, she bent
over to look into the tomb; 12and
she saw two angels in white,
sitting where the body of Jesus
had been lying, one at the head
and the other at the feet. 13They
said to her, "Woman, why are
you weeping?" She said to them,
"They have taken away my Lord,
and I do not know where they
have laid him." 14When she had
said this, she turned around and
saw Jesus standing there, but she
did not know that it was Jesus.
15Jesus said to her, "Woman,
why are you weeping? Whom
are you looking for?" Supposing
him to be the gardener, she said
to him, "Sir, if you have carried
him away, tell me where you
have laid him, and I will take
him away." 16Jesus said to her,
"Mary!" She turned and said to
him in Hebrew, "Rabbouni!"
(which means Teacher). 17Jesus
said to her, "Do not hold on
to me, because I have not yet
ascended to the Father. But go to
my brothers and say to them, 'I
am ascending to my Father and
your Father, to my God and your
God.'" 18Mary Magdalene went
and announced to the disciples,
"I have seen the Lord"; and she
told them that he had said these
things to her.

19When it was evening on that
day, the first day of the week,
and the doors of the house where
the disciples had met were locked
for fear of the Jews, Jesus came
and stood among them and said,
"Peace be with you." 20After he
said this, he showed them his
hands and his side. Then the
disciples rejoiced when they saw
the Lord. 21Jesus said to them
again, "Peace be with you. As

the Father has sent me, so I send you." [22]When he had said this, he breathed on them and said to them, "Receive the Holy Spirit. [23]If you forgive the sins of any, they are forgiven them; if you retain the sins of any, they are retained."

Reflection

Mary Magdalene has followed the other two disciples back to the tomb. But while they go inside, she stands outside the door of the tomb, weeping. She seems to feel alone in her grief, as if her search for the body of the Lord occupies her mind entirely.

She turns away from the tomb and sees Jesus standing there, but she does not know it is Jesus. Perhaps her vision is blurred as she looks through her tears, but she is determined to find the body of her Lord. She prepares to push past him to keep looking—Mary is absolutely preoccupied with her mission. "Sir, if you have carried him away, tell me where you have laid him, and I will take him away."

"Mary!"

Suddenly the spell is broken, and she knows that this is Jesus. By calling her name, he has told her that he knows her, and she replies with joy and excitement, "Rabbouni!" Normally, they might have embraced, but something about the newly resurrected body of Jesus means he is somehow not quite the same. Having grown up around the Chesapeake Bay, I am reminded of a soft-shell crab, newly emerged from its old shell, that is not yet ready to be touched, but this is just a human guess. There is still so much to learn about the resurrection of the body that we cannot know until it is time.

Jesus commissions Mary: Go and tell the other disciples a message from Jesus, "I am ascending to my Father and your Father, to my God and your God." So Mary goes and announces to the disciples, "I have seen the Lord," and she tells them what he has said. I imagine her laughing about how the body she was looking for found her!

The Rev. Dr. A. Katherine Grieb
The Meade Professor in Biblical Interpretation
at Virginia Theological Seminary
Alexandria, Virginia

Questions

What do we see through our tears? Grief or pain can be so overwhelming that the amazing reality of God's love for us in Jesus Christ can be temporarily blurred beyond recognition.

Mary Magdalene recognizes Jesus when he calls her by name. Can you recall an experience when someone called you by name at a time when you were vulnerable or in deep pain?

Prayer

Jesus, Lord of tenderness, in the midst of our tears, you call us by name and help us to recognize you in the midst of pain and grief. Open our eyes to see your redeeming work in our lives and in the world around us. Then send us to proclaim the good news of your love to our families and friends. We ask it in your Holy Name. *Amen.*

DAY 48

John 20:24-31

24But Thomas (who was called
the Twin), one of the twelve, was
not with them when Jesus came.
25So the other disciples told him,
"We have seen the Lord." But he
said to them, "Unless I see the
mark of the nails in his hands,
and put my finger in the mark
of the nails and my hand in his
side, I will not believe."

26A week later his disciples were
again in the house, and Thomas
was with them. Although the
doors were shut, Jesus came and
stood among them and said,
"Peace be with you." 27Then
he said to Thomas, "Put your
finger here and see my hands.
Reach out your hand and put
it in my side. Do not doubt but
believe." 28Thomas answered
him, "My Lord and my God!"
29Jesus said to him, "Have you
believed because you have seen
me? Blessed are those who have
not seen and yet have come to
believe." 30Now Jesus did many
other signs in the presence of his
disciples, which are not written
in this book. 31But these are
written so that you may come to
believe that Jesus is the Messiah,
the Son of God, and that
through believing you may have
life in his name.

Reflection

Thomas the Twin gets a bad rap as "Doubting Thomas." But remember John 11:16, where Jesus tells the disciples that he is going to return to Judea. His disciples point out that the Judeans have been trying to stone him. He can't be serious about going back there! It is Thomas who says to his fellow disciples, "Let us also go, that we may die with him." So why not "Brave Thomas" or "Loyal Thomas" or "True Disciple Thomas"? Perhaps the world is hard on Thomas because his approach to the news of Jesus' resurrection is something that we might have said. Thomas is one of those people who says out loud what others are actually already thinking. He is a great gift to us.

Thomas's request for physical proof of Jesus' bodily resurrection has often been understood as Thomas putting conditions that have to be met before he will believe the disciples. But another interpretation is that Thomas is concerned that someone might have deceived them. Only a three-dimensional examination would clarify that. In fact, Thomas is asking for nothing more than what the other disciples had already been given by Jesus himself.

I do not interpret Jesus' invitation to Thomas as a rebuke or a challenge, so much as an invitation to come close, to have his curiosity satisfied. Jesus knows what Thomas needs before Thomas asks him—and answers Thomas's request before it is even made. How often we discover that God knows what we need before we know it ourselves! Thomas's confession of faith is the last and best confession of faith in the gospel narrative. So why not "Believing Thomas"?

The Rev. Dr. A. Katherine Grieb
The Meade Professor in Biblical Interpretation
at Virginia Theological Seminary
Alexandria, Virginia

Questions

When in your life has doubt been a strength? When has doubt been the result of fear or inertia? How can you know the difference?

Prayer

Gracious and loving God, you know our needs before we ask, and you welcome us to bring our questions as we long to know you more deeply. Help us to be as brave as Thomas, bold enough to say what we think we need. Remind us, risen Lord, that you bear the marks of the cross even in your resurrection and that you invite us to meet you both in woundedness and in joy. Surround us, Spirit of power, with your gentle peace and the gift of assurance that in Jesus Christ our Lord, our sins are truly forgiven. In Jesus' name. *Amen.*

DAY 49

John 21:1-14

21 After these things Jesus showed himself again to the disciples by the Sea of Tiberias; and he showed himself in this way. 2Gathered there together were Simon Peter, Thomas called the Twin, Nathanael of Cana in Galilee, the sons of Zebedee, and two others of his disciples. 3Simon Peter said to them, "I am going fishing." They said to him, "We will go with you." They went out and got into the boat, but that night they caught nothing.

4Just after daybreak, Jesus stood on the beach; but the disciples did not know that it was Jesus. 5Jesus said to them, "Children, you have no fish, have you?" They answered him, "No." 6He said to them, "Cast the net to the right side of the boat, and you will find some." So they cast it, and now they were not able to haul it in because there were so many fish. 7That disciple whom Jesus loved said to Peter, "It is the Lord!" When Simon Peter heard that it was the Lord, he put on some clothes, for he was naked, and jumped into the sea. 8But the other disciples came in the boat, dragging the net full of fish, for they were not far from the land, only about a hundred yards off.

9When they had gone ashore, they saw a charcoal fire there, with fish on it, and bread. 10Jesus said to them, "Bring some of the fish that you have just caught." 11So Simon Peter went aboard and hauled the net ashore, full of large fish, a hundred fifty-three of them; and though there were so many, the net was not torn. 12Jesus said to them, "Come and have breakfast." Now none of the disciples dared to ask him, "Who are you?" because they knew it was the Lord. 13Jesus came and took the bread and gave it to them, and did the same with the fish. 14This was now the third time that Jesus appeared to the disciples after he was raised from the dead.

Reflection

Grieving is long, slow, hard work. Keeping busy and returning to normal tasks can aid in the grieving process. If we have no obligations and nothing to occupy ourselves with, our minds replay past conversations and events, and our grief can overwhelm us. Perhaps for this reason—and the need to support his family—Peter says, "I'm going fishing." The other disciples join him, including John, the son of Zebedee, for whom this gospel may have been named.

Unlike the other gospels where Jesus appears on a Galilean mountaintop after the crucifixion, John recounts Jesus appearing by the seaside. The disciples do not recognize him; perhaps the distance obscures their view or grief preoccupies them. When Jesus learns that they have fished all night and have caught nothing, he says, "Cast the net to the right side, and you will find some."

This detail is vital. Jews traditionally positioned their boats to where the River Jordan entered the Sea of Galilee. They cast their nets to the left, toward where the Jews lived—the kosher side of the great body of water. The disciples have followed tradition all night, with no success; Jesus urges them to try something different. So they break with tradition and toss their nets to the right side—where the Gentiles lived. Their nets are soon full of fish and nearly break. They catch 153 fish. It is a sign of the miraculous growth that the Church will soon experience as it focuses on evangelizing the Gentiles.

The Rev. Marek P. Zabriskie
Rector of St. Thomas' Episcopal Church
and Founder of The Bible Challenge
Fort Washington, Pennsylvania

Questions

Is God calling you to move in a different direction or handle something in a different way? Are you open to answers and suggestions that may be counterintuitive or go against your training and the traditions that you hold so dearly?

Prayer

Gracious God, you alone know what is best for our lives and where our efforts may be most fruitfully spent. Help us to hear your voice guiding us in new directions and to be willing to launch into the deep and take risks by carrying out our work in new and different ways. *Amen.*

DAY 50

John 21:15-25

15When they had finished
breakfast, Jesus said to Simon
Peter, "Simon son of John, do
you love me more than these?"
He said to him, "Yes, Lord; you
know that I love you." Jesus
said to him, "Feed my lambs."
16A second time he said to him,
"Simon son of John, do you love
me?" He said to him, "Yes, Lord;
you know that I love you." Jesus
said to him, "Tend my sheep."
17He said to him the third time,
"Simon son of John, do you love
me?" Peter felt hurt because he
said to him the third time, "Do
you love me?" And he said to him,
"Lord, you know everything; you
know that I love you." Jesus said
to him, "Feed my sheep. 18Very
truly, I tell you, when you were
younger, you used to fasten your
own belt and to go wherever you
wished. But when you grow old,
you will stretch out your hands,
and someone else will fasten a
belt around you and take you
where you do not wish to go."
19(He said this to indicate the
kind of death by which he would
glorify God.) After this he said to
him, "Follow me."

20Peter turned and saw the
disciple whom Jesus loved
following them; he was the one
who had reclined next to Jesus at
the supper and had said, "Lord,
who is it that is going to betray
you?" 21When Peter saw him, he
said to Jesus, "Lord, what about
him?" 22Jesus said to him, "If it
is my will that he remain until I
come, what is that to you? Follow
me!" 23So the rumor spread in
the community that this disciple
would not die. Yet Jesus did not
say to him that he would not
die, but, "If it is my will that he
remain until I come, what is that
to you?"

[24]This is the disciple who is testifying to these things and has written them, and we know that his testimony is true. [25]But there are also many other things that Jesus did; if every one of them were written down, I suppose that the world itself could not contain the books that would be written.

Reflection

We now transition from Jesus' resurrection to God's power to redeem each of us. Jesus has breakfast waiting for his disciples over a charcoal fire. This scene recalls when Peter stood with the slaves and priests by a charcoal fire before he denied Jesus three times (18:18-27).

Gathered now by a similar fire, Jesus asks Peter three times, "Do you love me more than these?" By the third time, Peter feels hurt—he realizes the connection between the three-fold questioning and his three-fold denial of Jesus.

A similar pattern occurs throughout the entire Bible, especially in Genesis 2-12, 2 Samuel 9-20, and 1 Kings 1-2. Adam and Eve, Cain and Abel, David and Bathsheba, and Amnon and Absalom inflict harm. In each of these stories, as in the story of Jesus and Peter, there is judgment, confession, forgiveness, and the offer of grace extended like a hand to a man who has fallen into a pit. A second chance is given.

Then Jesus instructs Peter, "When you grow old, you will stretch out your hands, and someone else will fasten a belt around you and take you where you do not wish to go." This foretells Peter's death. He will be crucified upside down outside of Rome around 64 CE. Jesus' final words in John's Gospel are, "Follow me," echoing his invitation for the disciples to "Come and see" in the first chapter. Much has transpired in the three years that separate these two invitations. The disciples now know that following Jesus is a costly endeavor, a commitment that will cost most of them their lives. They are now prepared to follow him.

The Rev. Marek P. Zabriskie
Rector of St. Thomas' Episcopal Church
and Founder of The Bible Challenge
Fort Washington, Pennsylvania

Questions

Are you prepared to follow Jesus come what may, cost what it will? What price are you paying to follow Jesus and to lead the Christian life? If God did not spare Jesus and the disciples from suffering, should we expect our loved ones and ourselves to live free of pain and suffering?

Prayer

Holy God, you have resurrected Jesus your only begotten Son in order that we might experience his risen life, be transformed and sent into the world to redeem others. May your healing and forgiving grace flow through us and give others the gift of a fresh start in life. *Amen.*

About the Authors

The Rev. Dr. Christopher A. Beeley is the Walter H. Gray Associate Professor of Anglican Studies and Patristics at the Berkeley Divinity School at Yale. He is the author and editor of several books, including *Leading God's People: Wisdom from the Early Church for Today* and *Gregory of Nazianzus on the Trinity and the Knowledge of God: In Your Light We Shall See Light,* which won a John Templeton Award for Theological Promise. (Days 7, 8)

The Rt. Rev. Thomas E. Breidenthal is the ninth bishop of the Episcopal Diocese of Southern Ohio. He has pastored or assisted congregations in Oregon; Oxford, England; and New York, as well as served as a high school chaplain. As an Episcopal Church Foundation Fellow, he studied at Oxford University, where he received a Doctor of Philosophy in Theology. He served as the John Henry Hobart Professor of Christian Ethics and Moral Theology at The General Theological Seminary in New York City from 1992-2001 and as Dean of Religious Life and of the Chapel at Princeton University (2001-2006). He is the author of *Christian Households and Sacred Unions* and was a contributor to *Soul Proclamations: Singing the Magnificat with Mary*, published by Forward Movement. He was a candidate for the 27th Presiding Bishop of The Episcopal Church. (Days 3, 4)

The Rev. Canon Professor Richard A. Burridge is dean of King's College London where he is also professor of biblical interpretation. He has written extensively on Jesus and the Gospels and how we use the Bible in ethics today. In 2013, he was awarded the Ratzinger Prize by Pope Francis, the only non-Catholic to be so honored to date. (Days 1,2)

The Rev. Dr. William J. Danaher Jr. is rector of Christ Church Cranbrook, where he has served since 2014. He also has served parishes in Connecticut, New York City, Tennessee, and Ontario. He received his M.Div. from Virginia Theological Seminary and his Ph.D. from Yale University. He was associate professor of Theology and Ethics at the University of the South (Sewanee, Tennessee) from 2000-2006, associate professor of moral theology in the John Henry Hobart Chair at The General Theological Seminary in New York City from 2006-2008, and dean of the faculty of theology and the Huron-Lawson Chair in Moral and Pastoral Theology at Huron University College in London, Ontario, from 2008-2014. (Days 35, 36)

The Very Rev. Peter Jay DeVeau is dean of Grace & Holy Trinity Cathedral, Kansas City, Missouri. He also has served congregations in Springfield, Missouri, and Seattle, Washington. A native of the Diocese of New York, DeVeau studied for ordained ministry at Berkeley Divinity School at Yale and received an M.Div. in 1986. He is a strong advocate for the formation of adults through the Catechumenate and the development of cathedrals as resource centers. (Days 37, 38)

The Rev. Christopher L. Epperson is the rector of Bruton Parish Church in Williamsburg, Virginia. He has served parishes in Tennessee, Atlanta, and Rhode Island. He is an avid reader, cyclist, and traveler. (Days 29, 30)

The Rev. Lindsay Hardin Freeman is a Minnesota-based Episcopal priest and the writer/editor of eight books. She has won over thirty awards for journalistic excellence, including the 2015 Gold Medal Award in Bible Study from Independent Publishers for her recent book, *Bible Women: All Their Words and Why They Matter,* published by Forward Movement. Currently serving as adjunct clergy at St. David's, Minnetonka, Minnesota, she has also served congregations in Boston and Philadelphia. (Days 19, 20)

The Rev. Dr. Paul D. Fromberg is the rector of St. Gregory of Nyssa Episcopal Church in San Francisco, California. In addition to his congregational ministry, he is an adjunct instructor in practical theology at the Church Divinity School of the Pacific and teaches liturgics for the Diocese of Minnesota. He is the author of the forthcoming book, *The Art of Transformation*. (Days 43, 44)

Dr. Greg Garrett is the author of over twenty books of fiction, memoir, and theology, including the recent *My Church Is Not Dying: Episcopalians in the 21st Century.* He frequently speaks, preaches, and leads retreats across the United States and overseas. He is a professor of English at Baylor University and writer in residence at the Seminary of the Southwest in Austin, Texas, where he lives with his wife, Jeanie, and their family. (Days 25, 26)

The Rev. Dr. David T. Gortner is associate dean of church and community engagement at Virginia Theological Seminary, where he directs the doctor of ministry program, teaches evangelism and congregational and community development, and works with congregations and community organizations across the mid-Atlantic region and the United States. He has degrees from Wheaton College, Wake Forest University, Seabury-Western Theological Seminary, and the University of Chicago. He is the author of several books, including *Transforming Evangelism, Around One Table,* and *Varieties of Personal Theology.* (Days 23, 24)

The Rev. Dr. Gordon Graham is the Henry Luce III Professor of Philosophy and the Arts at Princeton Theological Seminary and priest associate at All Saints' Episcopal Church in Princeton, New Jersey. He has published many papers on philosophical, theological, and ethical topics, and his books include *Evil and Christian Ethics.* (Days 5, 6)

The Rev. Dr. A. Katherine Grieb has taught New Testament at Virginia Theological Seminary since 1994. She is currently the Meade Professor in Biblical Interpretation. She serves part-time at St. Stephen and the Incarnation Episcopal Church in Washington, D.C. A popular preacher and teacher, she leads retreats and Bible studies for diocesan clergy days and other church groups. She has authored many articles and book chapters related to the New Testament, theological interpretation of scripture, and preaching, including *The Story of Romans.* (Days 47, 48)

The Rt. Rev. Daniel G. P. Gutierrez is the bishop of the Episcopal Diocese of Pennsylvania. He previously served as canon to the ordinary, chief operating officer, and chief of staff for the Diocese of the Rio Grande. He also served The Episcopal Church through administrative and budgetary oversight of the Navajoland Area Mission and was vice president of The Episcopal Church in Navajoland Economic Development Corporation. Prior to that, he served as chief of staff to the mayor of Albuquerque and was president of a strategy and media firm whose clients included state and local political leaders. He earned a diocesan certificate in Anglican studies through the Trinity School for Ministry, and in 2011, he was awarded a master of theological studies degree from St. Norbert College. (Days 31, 32)

The Very Rev. Lucinda Laird is dean of the American Cathedral in Paris. She is a native of New Orleans, Louisiana, and a graduate of Barnard College (Columbia University) and The General Theological Seminary. Before moving to France, she served parishes in the dioceses of New York, Newark, and Kentucky. (Days 27, 28)

The Very Rev. Justin Lindstrom is the dean of St. Paul's Cathedral in Oklahoma City. He is a community leader and dynamic preacher who enjoys time with his family and travel. You will often find Justin reading, running, or sipping a cup of coffee in a local cafe. (Days 39, 40)

The Rt. Rev. Carlos López-Lozano is the bishop of the Reformed Episcopal Church of Spain. He was consecrated by the Archbishop of Canterbury in 1995. He has degrees from the Pontifical University of Salamanca and his Ph.D. from the University Ovidius of Constanta. He was a member of the central committee of the World Council of Churches and a member of the Anglican Consultative Counsel. (Days 33, 34)

The Rev. John Ohmer is the rector of The Falls Church Episcopal in Falls Church, Virginia. He is a graduate of Wabash College and Virginia Theological Seminary. He blogs at Unapologetic Theology and is the author of the book, *Slaying Your Goliaths: How God Can Help*, published by Forward Movement. (Days 13, 14)

The Rt. Rev. Jacob W. Owensby is the fourth bishop of the Episcopal Diocese of Western Louisiana. He blogs at Pelican Anglican. His latest book is *Gospel Memories: The Future Can Rewrite the Past.* (Days 11, 12)

The Very Rev. Dr. Martyn Percy is the dean of Christ Church, Oxford, one of the University of Oxford's largest colleges, as well as the Cathedral Church of the Diocese of Oxford. From 2004-2014, he was principal of Ripon College, Cuddesdon, a leading Anglican seminary in the Church of England. He writes on ecclesiology and spirituality, and his recent books include *An Anglican Landscape of Faith: Thirty-Nine New Articles, The Bright Field,* and *Darkness Yielding.* (Days 17, 18)

The Rev. Gideon L. K. Pollach serves as rector of St. John's Church, Cold Spring Harbor, in the Diocese of Long Island. He served for several years as head chaplain at the Episcopal High School in Alexandria, Virginia, and has worked in parishes in Virginia and New York. His ministry is inspired by the "mission statement" of the Gospel of Mark 1:15: "The time is fulfilled, the Kingdom of God has come near, repent and believe the good news." (Days 21, 22)

The Rev. Canon Isaac Poobalan serves as provost and rector of St. Andrew's Cathedral in Aberdeen, Scotland, where Samuel Seabury, the first bishop for The Episcopal Church, was consecrated. Born and raised in South India, Poobalan served in Desert Storm as part of the Allied Forces in liberating Kuwait. He retired from active service to train for the sacred ministry in the Scottish Episcopal Church. He is married to Amu, an obesity epidemiologist at the University of Aberdeen, and they have two children. (Days 41, 42)

The Rev. Minka S. Sprague is director of the Chapel of the Holy Spirit, the Episcopal and Evangelical Lutheran Church of America campus ministry to Tulane and Loyola universities. She previously served as deacon at St. James' Episcopal Church in Jackson,

Mississippi. Prior to that, she served as professor of New Testament and biblical languages at New York Theological Seminary and deacon at the Cathedral of St. John the Divine. She is also the author of *Praying from the Free-Throw Line—for Now.* She resides in New Orleans. (Days 9, 10)

Dr. Jenny Te Paa-Daniel received her Ph.D. from Graduate Theological Union in Berkeley, California. She is a globally experienced teacher, public theologian, social justice activist, and lay Anglican indigenous woman. She lives and works in Auckland, New Zealand, and Aitutaki, Cook Islands. (Days 15, 16)

The Rev. Lucy Winkett is rector of St James's Church, Piccadilly, and served previously as canon precentor of St. Paul's Cathedral, London. With degrees in history and theology and as a trained soprano, she is much in demand as a speaker, writer, and musician. She broadcasts regularly on national radio in the United Kingdom and is the author of *Our Sound is our Wound*, which was the Archbishop of Canterbury's Lent book for 2010. (Days 45, 46)

The Rev. Marek P. Zabriskie has served as the rector of St. Thomas' Episcopal Church in Fort Washington, Pennsylvania, for more than twenty years, and served churches in Virginia and Tennessee prior to that. He is the founder and director of the Center for Biblical Studies, which promotes The Bible Challenge, which he created, to Christians and seekers in more than fifty countries. Currently, more than 500,000 Christians in over 2,500 churches have participated. He is also the editor of The Bible Challenge books and author of *Doing the Bible Better: The Bible Challenge and the Transformation of the Episcopal Church.* To learn more about The Bible Challenge, visit www.thecenterforbiblicalstudies.org. (Days 49, 50)

About Forward Movement

Forward Movement is committed to inspiring disciples and empowering evangelists. While we produce great resources like this book, Forward Movement is not a publishing company. We are a ministry.

Our mission is to support you in your spiritual journey, to help you grow as a follower of Jesus Christ. Publishing books, daily reflections, studies for small groups, and online resources is an important way that we live out this ministry. More than a half million people read our daily devotions through *Forward Day by Day*, which is also available in Spanish (*Adelante Día a Día*) and Braille, online, as a podcast, and as an app for your smartphones or tablets. It is mailed to more than fifty countries, and we donate nearly 30,000 copies each quarter to prisons, hospitals, and nursing homes. We actively seek partners across the Church and look for ways to provide resources that inspire and challenge.

A ministry of The Episcopal Church for eighty years, Forward Movement is a nonprofit organization funded by sales of resources and gifts from generous donors. To learn more about Forward Movement and our resources, please visit us at www.forwardmovement.org (or www.venadelante.org).

We are delighted to be doing this work and invite your prayers and support.